HIGH SCHOOL BASEBALL RULES SIMPLIFIED & ILLUSTRATED 2018

ROBERT B. GARDNER, Publisher
B. Elliot Hopkins, Editor
NFHS Publications

To maintain the sound traditions of this sport, encourage sportsmanship and minimize the inherent risk of injury, the National Federation of State High School Associations writes playing rules for varsity competition among student-athletes of high school age. High school coaches, officials and administrators who have knowledge and experience regarding this particular sport and age group volunteer their time to serve on the rules committee. Member associations of the NFHS independently make decisions regarding compliance with or modification of these playing rules for the student-athletes in their respective states.

NFHS rules are used by education-based and non-education-based organizations serving children of varying skill levels who are of high school age and younger. In order to make NFHS rules skill-level and age-level appropriate, the rules may be modified by any organization that chooses to use them. Except as may be specifically noted in this rules book, the NFHS makes no recommendation about the nature or extent of the modifications that may be appropriate for children who are younger or less skilled than high school varsity athletes.

Every individual using these rules is responsible for prudent judgment with respect to each contest, athlete and facility, and each athlete is responsible for exercising caution and good sportsmanship. These rules should be interpreted and applied so as to make reasonable accommodations for disabled athletes, coaches and officials.

2018 High School Baseball Rules Simplified & Illustrated

Produced by Referee Enterprises Inc., publishers of Referee magazine.

Published by the
NATIONAL FEDERATION
OF STATE HIGH SCHOOL ASSOCIATIONS
PO Box 690
Indianapolis, IN 46206
Phone: 317-972-6900, Fax: 317.822.5700
www.nfhs.org

ISBN-13: 978-1-58208-377-3

Printed in the United States of America

Table of Contents

When the illustrations and statements do not give the complete answer, check the baseball rules book and case book for the technicalities. This book would not be simple if it covered all facets of the rules.

Requests for baseball rules interpretations or explanations should be directed to the state association responsible for the high school baseball program in your state. The NFHS will assist in answering rules questions from state associations whenever called upon.

2018 NFHS Baseball Rules Changes

Rule Changed

1-3-1 .... Added that balls must meet the current NOCSAE standard for baseballs effective Jan. 1, 2019.

1-3-2a2 .... Added that bats shall not have attachments that would present a potential hazard.

1-5-3 .... Added that the catcher's chest protector shall meet the NOCSAE standard effective Jan. 1, 2020.

8-2-7 .... The batter-runner may overrun or overslide first base on a base on balls.

2018 NFHS Editorial Changes

Editorial changes were made to 1-3-2b3, 2-21-1c, 5-1-2f, Dead Ball and Delayed Dead Ball Table.

Points of Emphasis

1. Sportsmanship: national anthem standoff and bench jockeying, celebrations and negative comments between opponents

2. Enforcement of NFHS jewelry rule

3. Enforcement and administration of NFHS rules

4. Proper pitching positions

Part 1

2018 New or Revised NFHS Rules

This simplified and illustrated book is a supplement to the 2018 NFHS Baseball Rules Book. As such, it is intended to aid in the administration of the game and in the standardization of interpretations through a unique method of presenting rules.

Each year, the NFHS Baseball Rules Committee considers many items which are submitted as potential changes or revisions. The items which secured favorable endorsement are listed on the previous page of this book. The majority of illustrations in Part 1 show these changes and revisions.

The NFHS Baseball Rules Committee also identified areas of concern which are designated as "Points of Emphasis" for the current season. They appear in Part 2. However, no rule changes were made to cover those particular items.

The illustrations found in Part 3 of this book have been revised to reflect any changes or clarifications as directed by the committee. Recent interpretations have been added to keep the contents current.

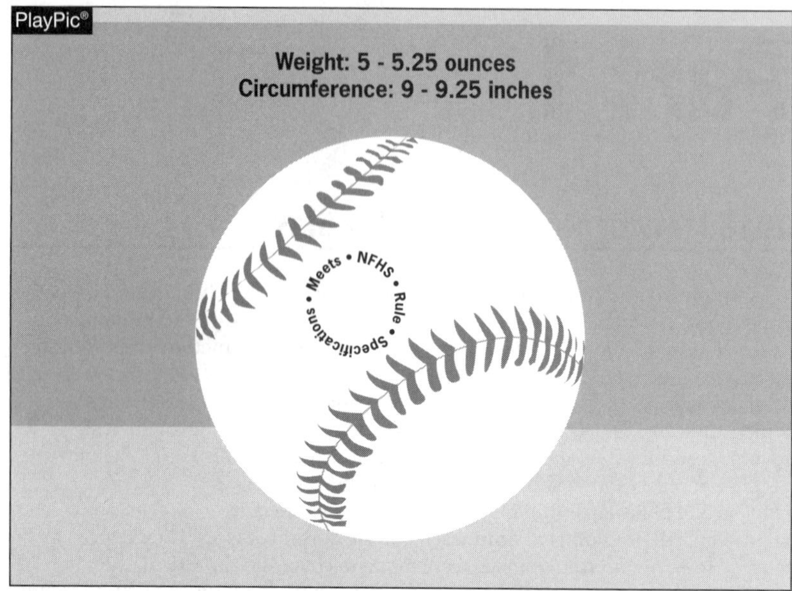

1-3-1 The ball shall meet the current NOCSAE standard for baseballs (effective Jan. 1, 2019).

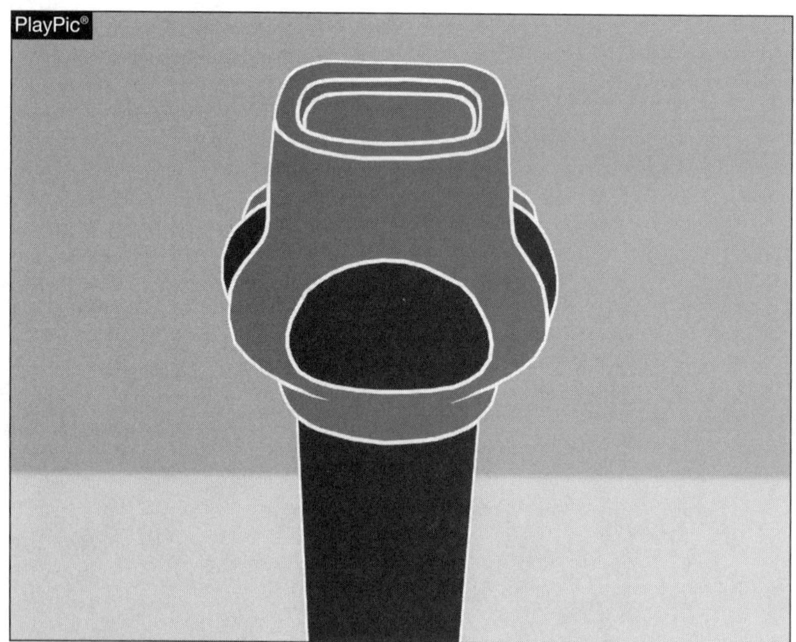

1-3-2a2 Bats shall not have exposed rivets, pins, rough or sharp edges or any form of exterior fastener or attachments that would present a potential hazard.

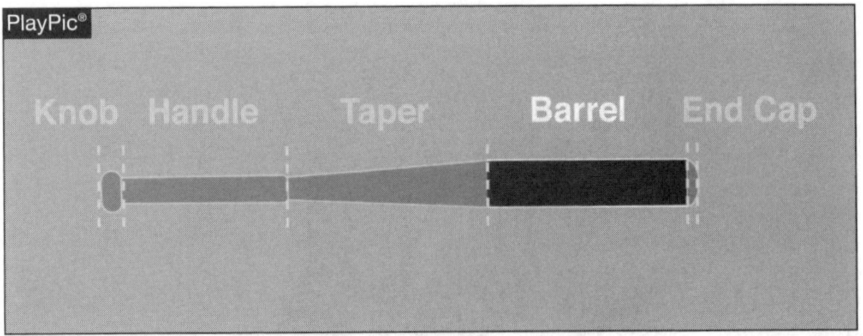

1-3-2b3 The barrel is the area intended for contact with a pitched ball. The rulebook language was updated for editorial clarity.

PlayPic®

1-5-3 The catcher's chest protector shall meet the NOCSAE standard (effective Jan. 1, 2020).

2-21c, 5-1-2f Rule language was updated to better reflect the 2017 rule change regarding a coach physically assisting a runner during playing action. If a runner is physically assisted by a coach, the runner is called out immediately and the ball remains live.

8-2-7 A batter-runner who reached first base safety and then overruns or overslides may immediately return without liability of being put out provided he does not attempt or feint an advance to second. This now applies to a player who is awarded first base on a base on balls.

Part 2

2018 NFHS Points of Emphasis

1. Sportsmanship — National Anthem Standoff

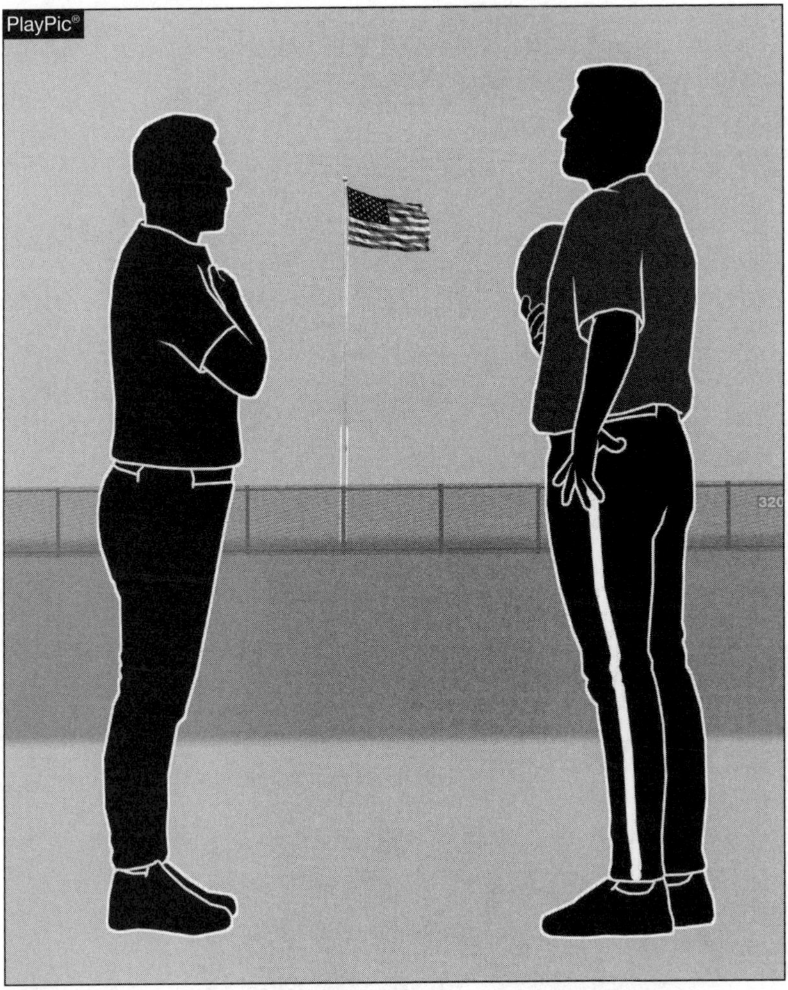

National anthem standoffs do not reflect education-based athletics. Staring down opponents after the national anthem to try to intimidate them or refusing to leave the respective baseline before the other team departs is juvenile and disrespectful.

2. Sportsmanship — Bench Jockeying and Celebrations

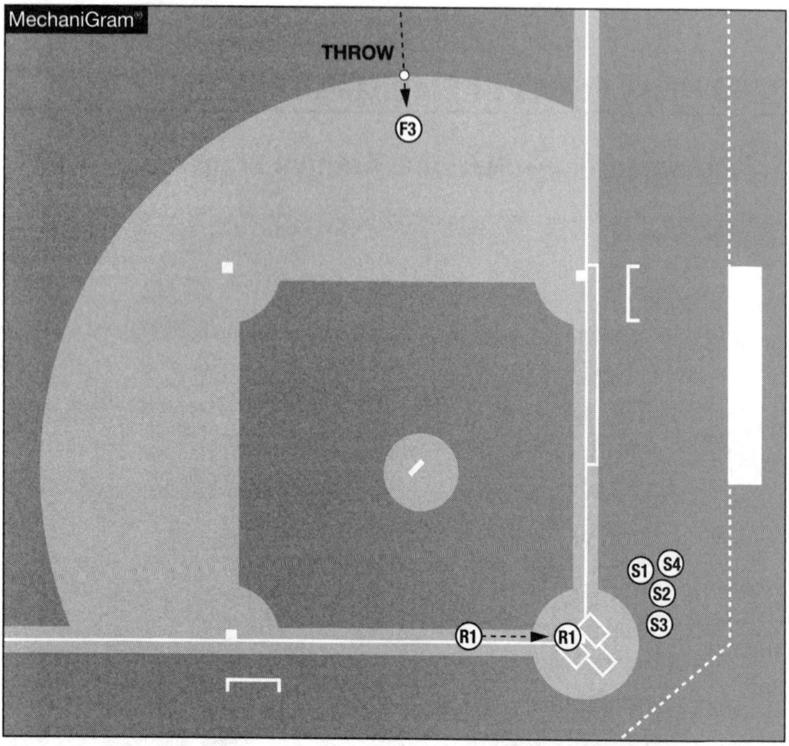

Coaches, players, substitutes, attendants or other bench personnel shall not leave the dugout during a live ball for any unauthorized purposes.

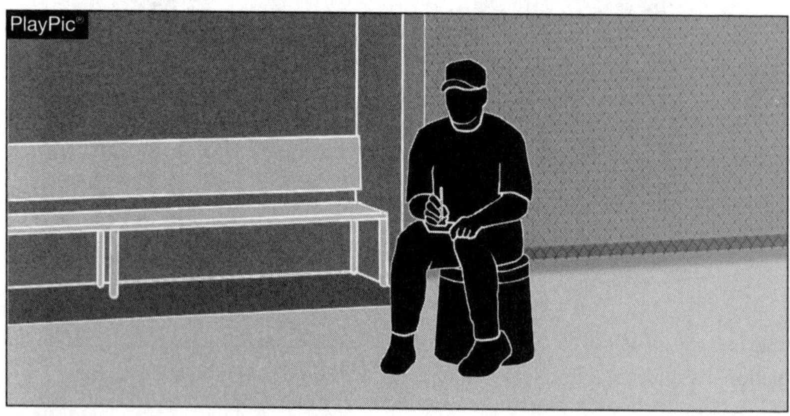

Coaches or team personnel may not sit outside the dugout/bench area on buckets or stools.

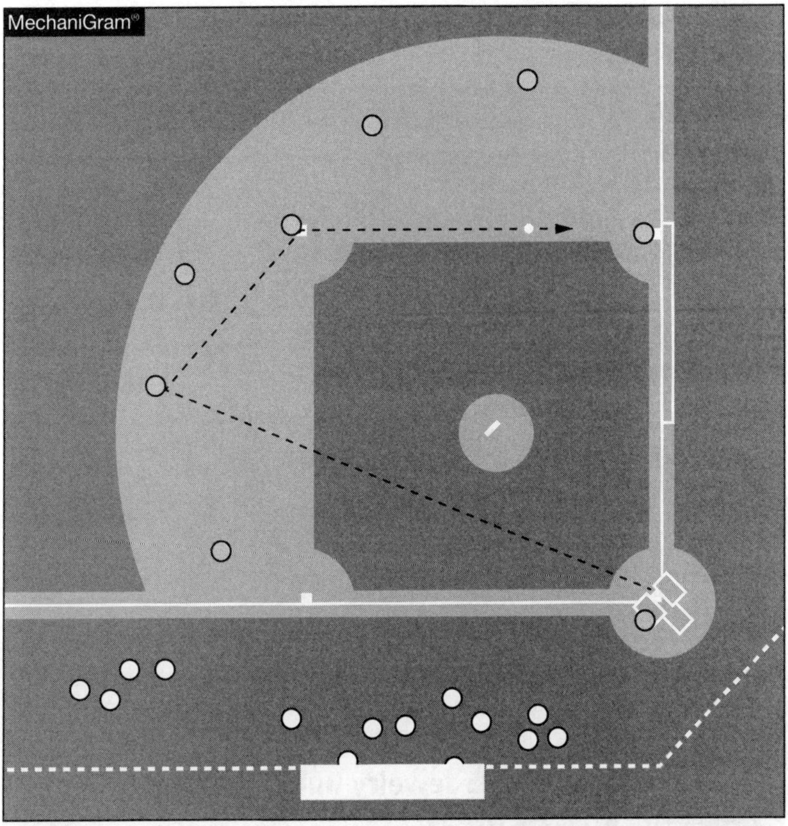

MechaniGram®

Players are not allowed to stand outside their dugout/bench area and make "cat-calls" or other disparaging remarks while the other team is taking infield practice.

3. Sportsmanship — Negative Comments Between Opponents

Chants, intentional distractions and loud noises directed at the opponent's pitcher prior to his pitching, the batter getting ready to hit, or a fielder getting ready to make a play do not represent good sportsmanship.

4. Enforcement of NFHS Jewelry Rule

Jewelry — including necklaces, bracelets and earrings — shall not be worn except for religious or medical medals. A religious medal must be taped and worn under the uniform. A medical alert must be taped and may be visible.

5. Enforcement and Administration of NFHS Rules

The rules of high school baseball are designed for the age and skill level of high school players and best serve education-based athletics. Use of non-approved interpretations or rulings that are contradictory to NFHS rules as written can confuse students, coaches, umpires and fans.

6. Proper Pitching Positions

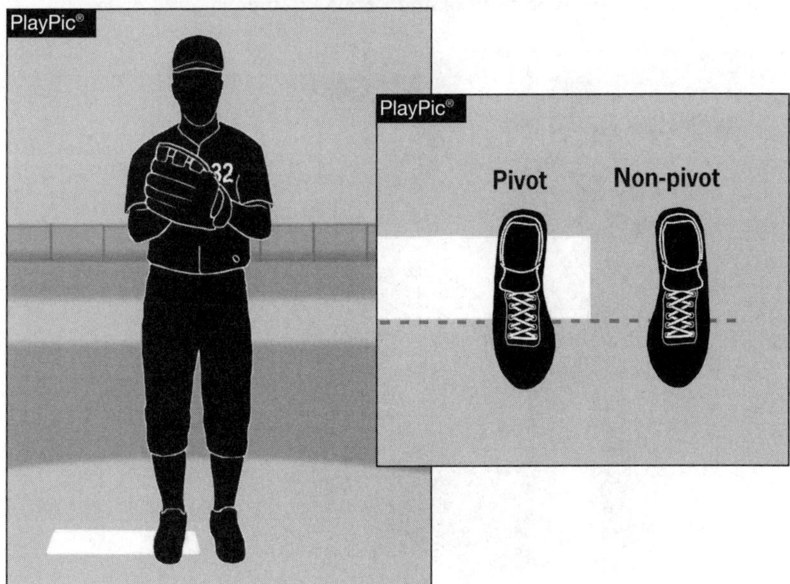

The windup is the second of two legal pitching positions. For the windup, the pitcher's non-pivot foot shall be in any position on or behind a line extending through the front edge of the pitcher's plate.

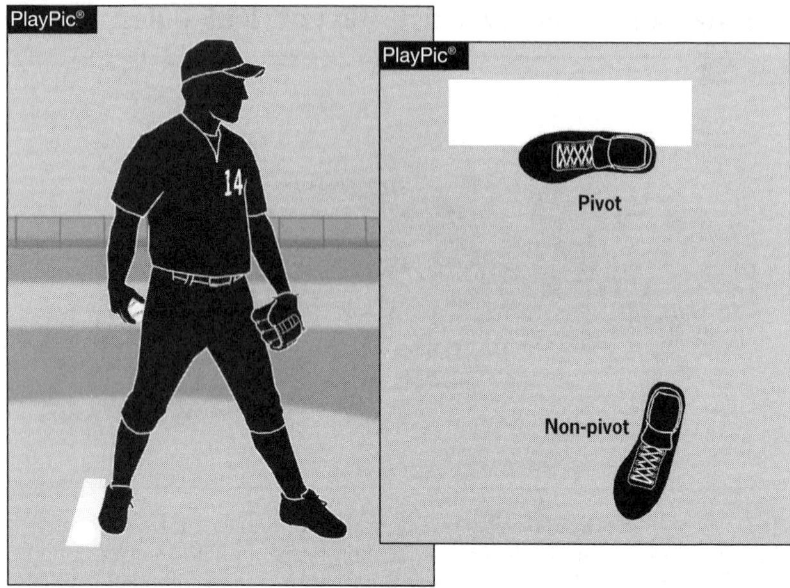

The set is one of two legal pitching positions. For the set position, a pitcher shall stand with his entire non-pivot foot in front of a line extending through the front edge of the pitcher's plate and with his entire pivot foot in contact with or directly in front of and parallel to the pitcher's plate.

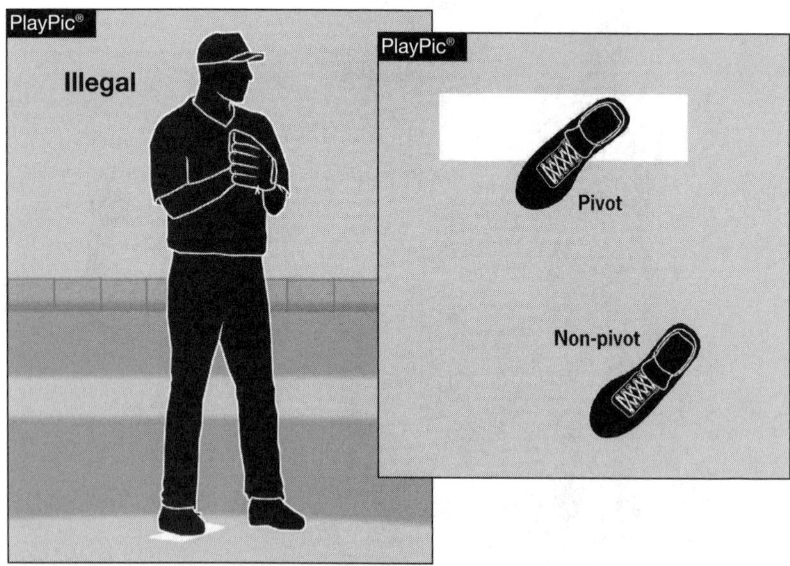

The so-called hybrid stance is illegal as it does not meet the requirements of either the windup or set positions.

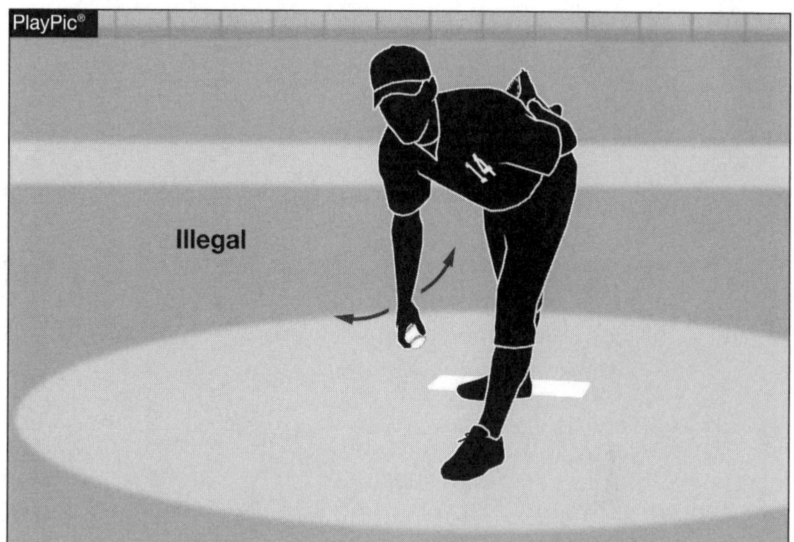

While in the set position, pitchers may dangle their arm in front, but they may not rock their arm from side to side. Any movement of the arm is considered the start of the pitching motion and a pitch must be delivered to the plate. As a result, that motion results in a balk.

Going to the mouth while in contact with the pitcher's plate is a balk, not because the pitcher goes to his mouth, but because the action simulates the start of the pitching motion.

Part 3
Rule 1

Players – Field and Equipment

The most basic rule of baseball is the first in the book: "Each team is permitted seven turns at bat during which it attempts to score runs by having its batters become base runners who advance … to the plate. The team in the field attempts to end each turn at bat of the opponent by causing three … to be out."

The first section of the rules deals with the field on which the game is played and the equipment that is used by all players.

Unlike other sports, where the court or field size and the equipment are standard throughout, baseball fields can be vastly different in outfield size, but the infields are always a 90-foot square. The equipment that players use also vary widely, as different participants prefer various size gloves and bats.

With all of the possible differences, the Baseball Rules Committee has instituted limits as to the size of equipment to ensure an equal balance between offense and defense.

1-1-2 Each team's head coach and captains (if available) shall attend the pregame plate meeting with the umpires.

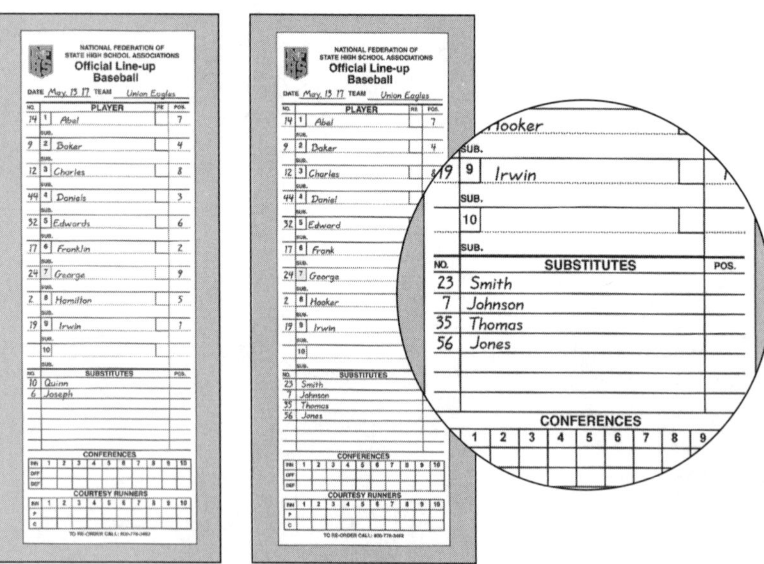

1-1-2 The name and shirt number of each eligible and available substitute should be listed on the lineup card. There is no penalty if substitutes are not listed.

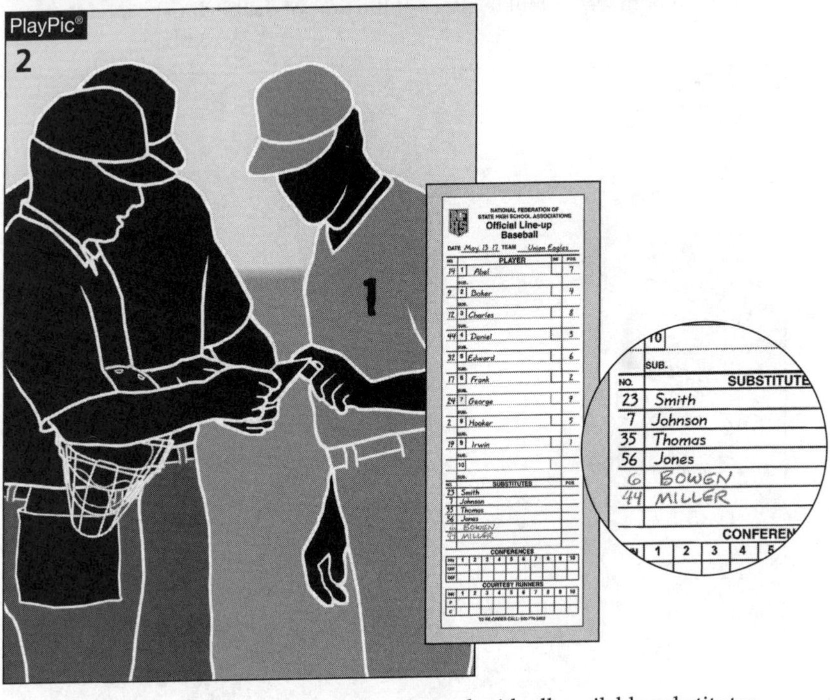

1-1-2 The head coach shall submit a lineup card with all available substitutes at the pregame conference (PlayPic 1). There is no penalty for adding substitute players during a game. In the third inning, two players have been added by the umpire-in-chief (PlayPic 2). The new rule is designed to make the substitution process more smooth, not to penalize.

1-1-4 The first baseman, shown holding the runner on base, is considered to be in fair ground, since he has at least one foot in fair ground. The first baseman would need both feet in foul territory at the time of the pitch to be in violation of this rule.

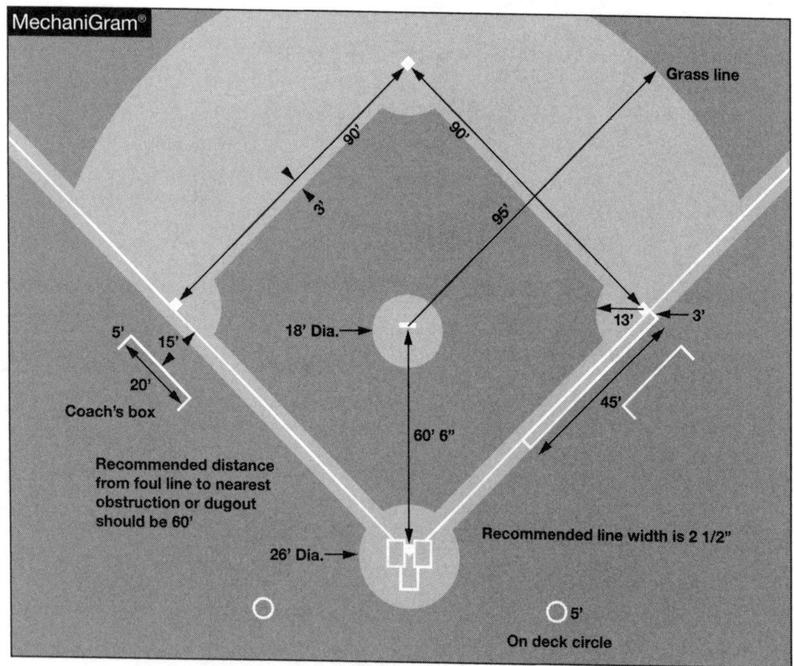

1-2-1 A diamond (or infield) shall be a 90-foot square. When measuring the distance to first base and third base, measure from the apex of the plate to the back edge of the base. The outfield is the area between two foul lines formed by extending two sides of the diamond.

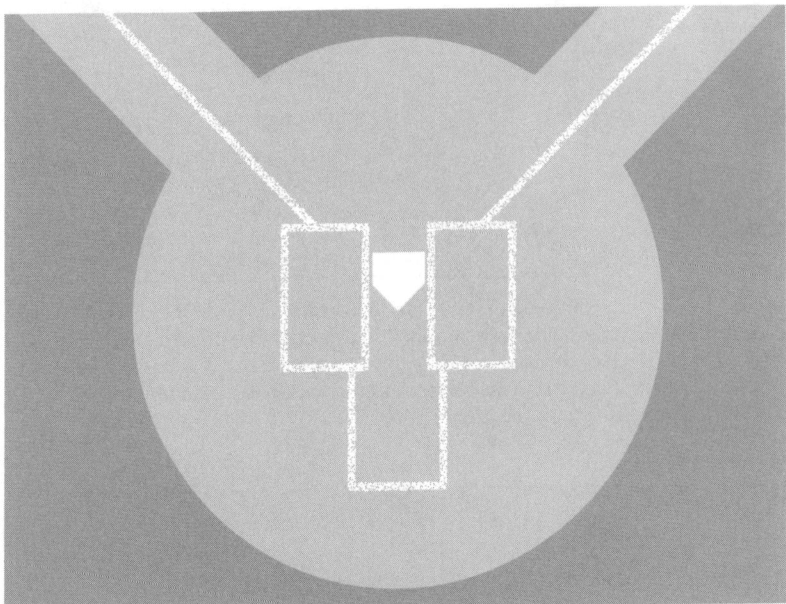

1-2-2 Non-permanent lines on the playing field shall be white in color. If lines are permanent, such as on artificial turf, non-white lines are legal.

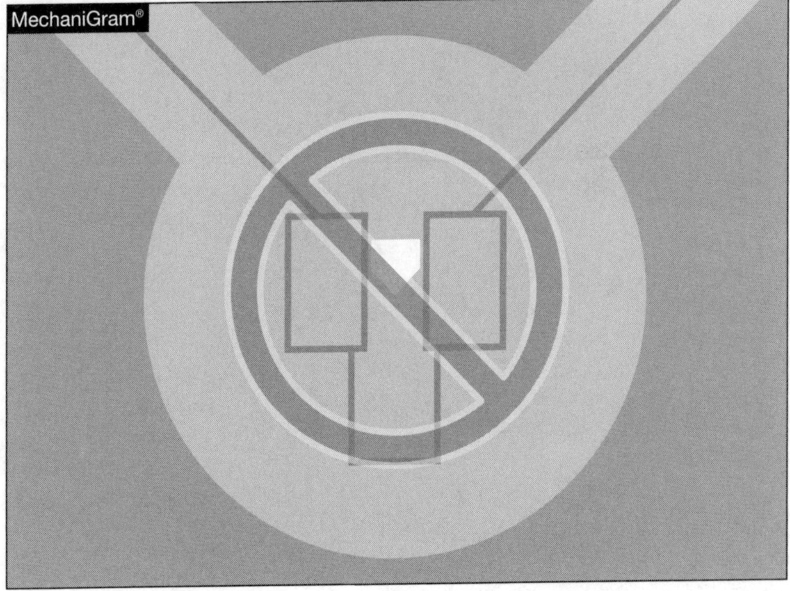

1-2-2 Non-permanent lines must be white so that there is a clear contrast between the lines and the color of the field. Umpires must be able to see the lines in order to make proper rulings.

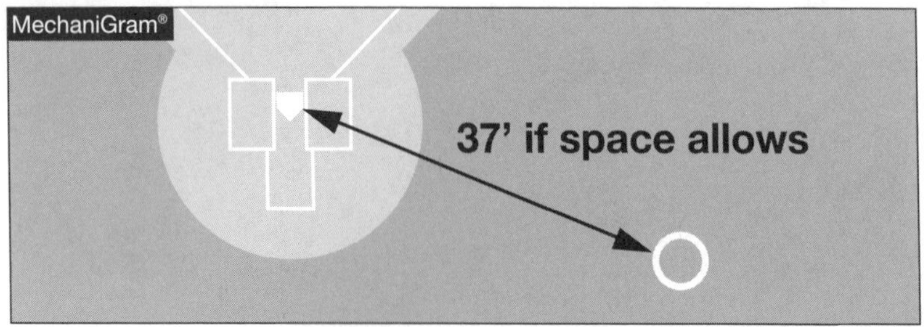

1-2-3 The on-deck circle should be to the side and away from the plate, 37 feet if space allows. Neither team's players shall warm up in the other team's on-deck circle. The on-deck circle does not have to be occupied, but if a player wishes to warm up, he shall do so only in his team's on-deck circle, provided the on-deck circle is located safely away from the plate.

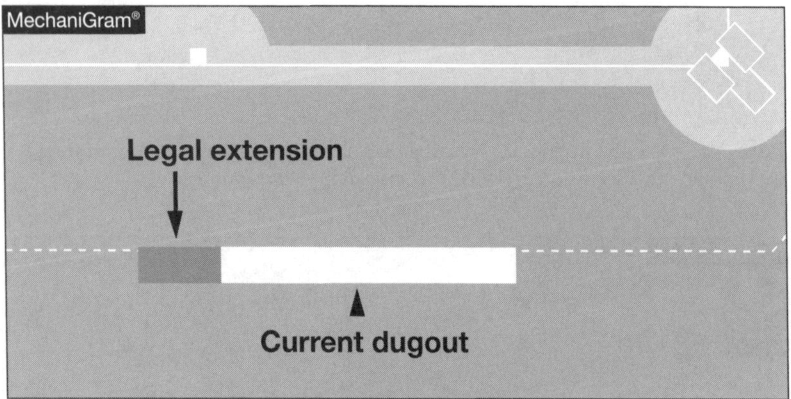

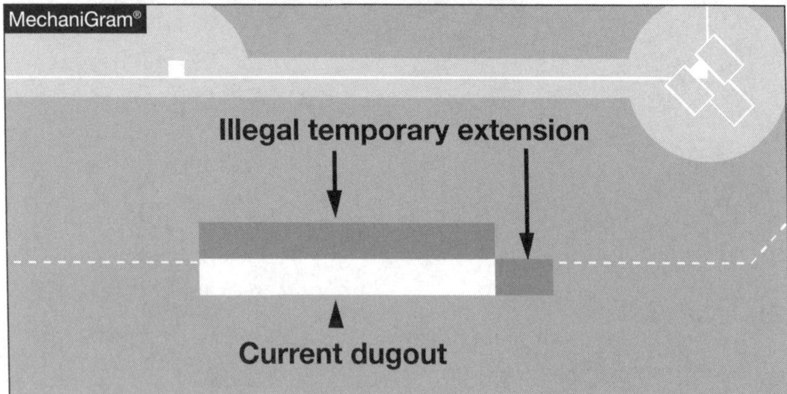

1-2-4 Teams may not temporarily extend the dugout any closer toward the plate. Teams may only extend the dugout in a direction away from the plate and in line with the current dugout.

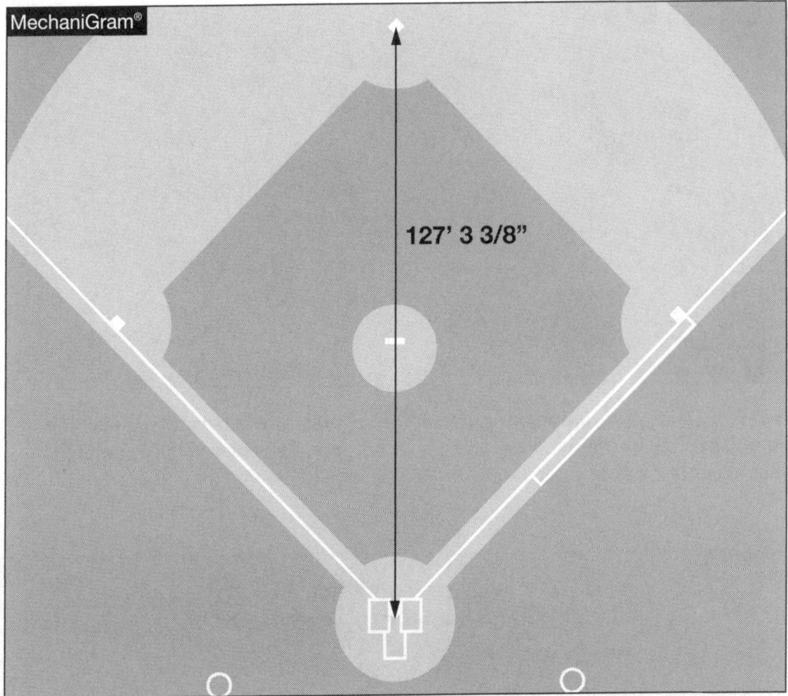

1-2-5 The distance from the rear tip of the plate to the middle of second base is 127 feet, 3 3/8 inches.

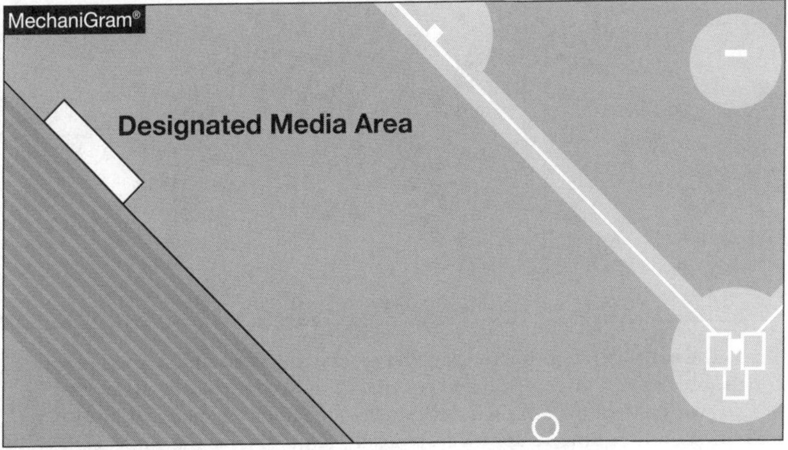

1-2-8 Game management is not required to mark off a designated media area, but must do so before the game starts if it wants to permit photographers on the field during the game. If an area is not designated and marked, media are prohibited from being on the field throughout the game.

1-2-9 By state association adoption, a double first base is permitted. The double first base shall be a white base and a colored base. The colored base shall be located entirely in foul territory.

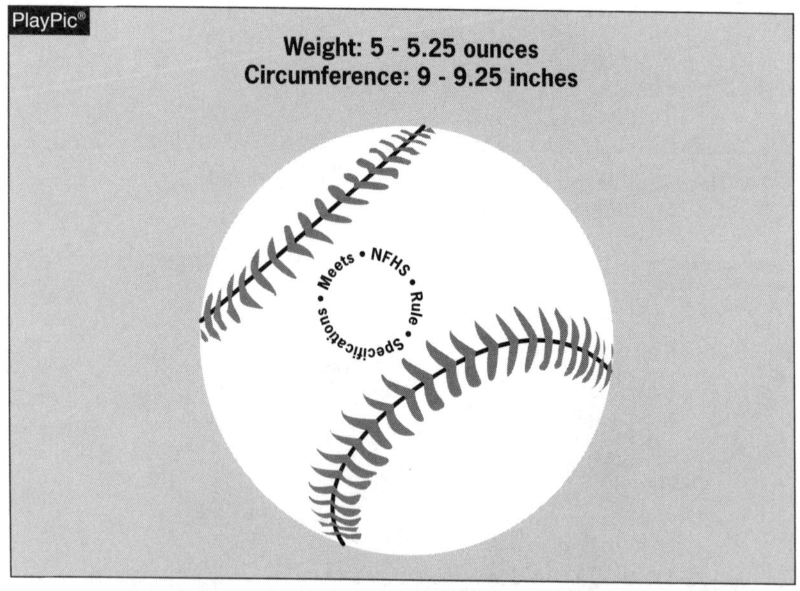

1-3-1 The ball shall be a sphere formed by yarn wound around a small core of cork, rubber or similar material and covered with two strips of white horsehide or two strips of white cowhide tightly stitched together. Teams must furnish a minimum of three umpire-approved baseballs at the start of the game. Unless otherwise mutually agreed upon, the home team has this responsibility. The NFHS Authenticating Mark is required on all balls that will be used in high school competition. A current list of NFHS authenticated products can be found on the Web site: www.nfhs.org. Effective Jan. 1, 2019, the ball shall meet the current NOCSAE standard for baseballs.

1-3-2 To be considered a wood bat, a bat must be a single piece of wood. All other bats must meet BBCOR standards. Examples of such non-wood bats that must meet BBCOR standards are those made of bamboo or those with metal handles and wood barrels.

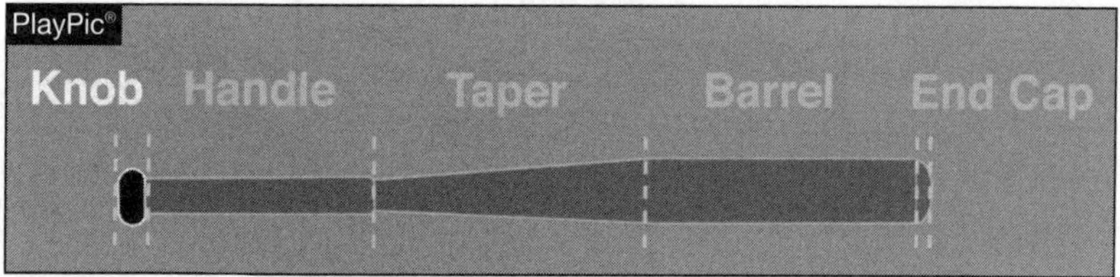

1-3-2b The bat knob shall protrude from the handle. It may be molded, lathed, welded or permanently fastened. Devices, attachments or wrappings are permitted except those that cause the knob to become flush with the handle. A one-piece rubber knob and bat grip combination is illegal.

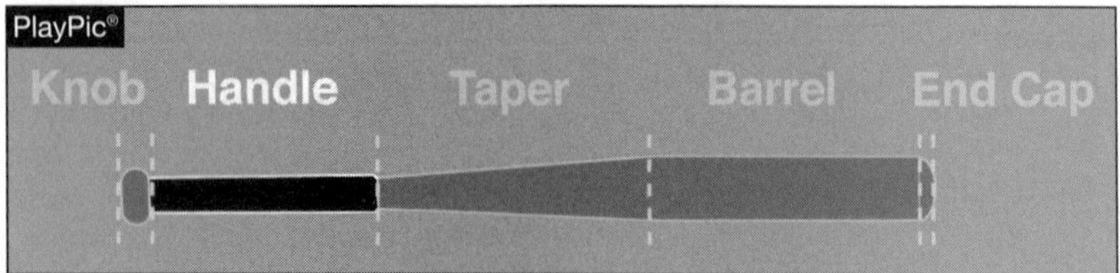

1-3-2b The bat handle is the area of the bat that begins at, but does not include, the knob and ends where the taper begins. There are no restrictions on the shape of the handle.

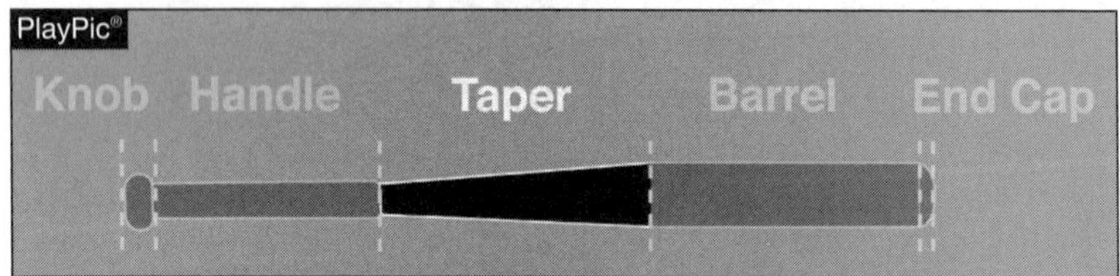

1-3-2b The taper is an optional transition area which connects the narrower handle to the wider barrel portion of the bat. Its length and material may vary but may not extend more than 18 inches from the base of the knob.

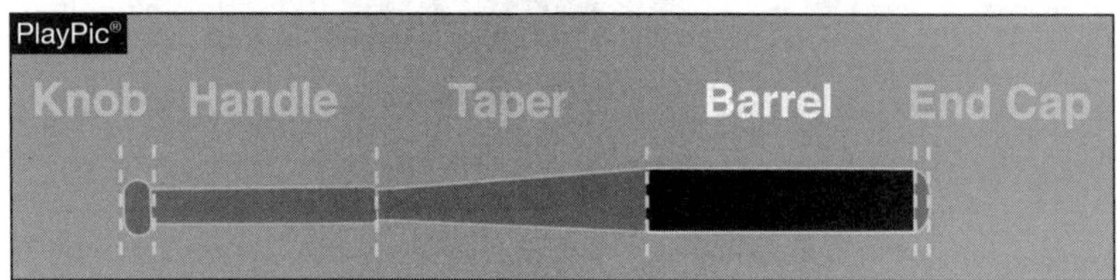

1-3-2b The barrel is the area intended for contact with the pitched ball. It shall be round, cylindrically symmetric and smooth. The barrel may be aluminum, wood or composite (made of two or more materials). The type of bat (wood, aluminum or composite) shall be determined by the composition of the barrel.

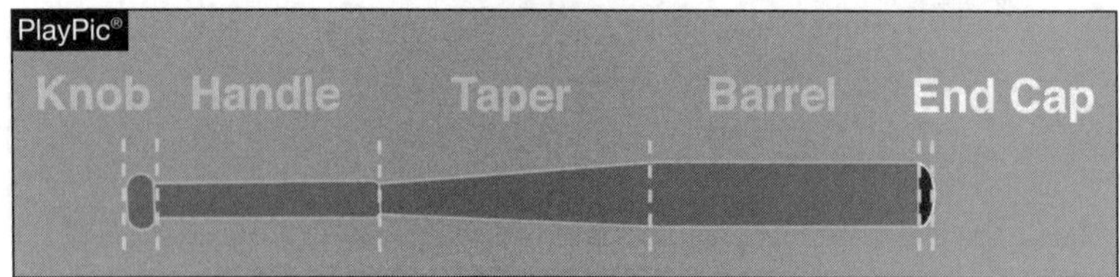

1-3-2b The end cap is made of rubber, vinyl, plastic or other approved material. It shall be firmly secured and permanently affixed to the end of the bat so that it cannot be removed by anyone other than the manufacturer, without damaging or destroying it. By definition, a one-piece construction bat does not have an end cap.

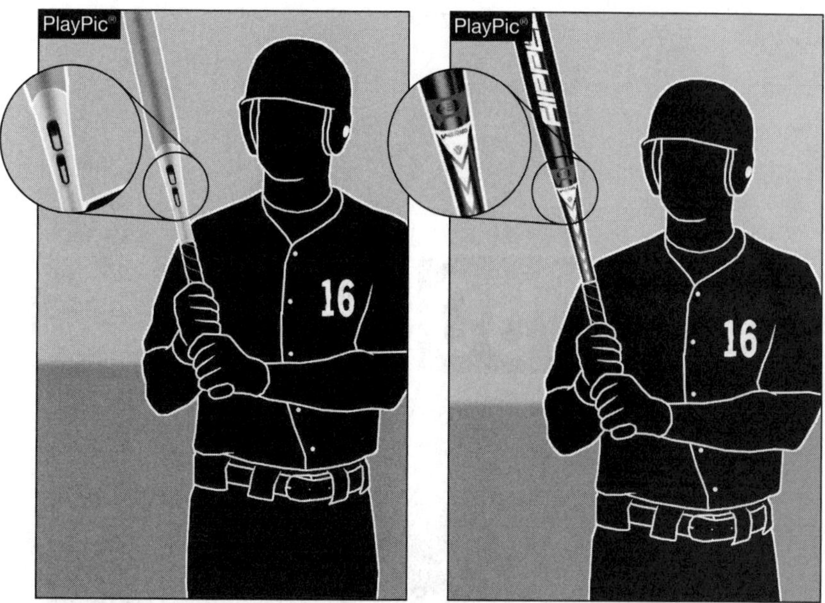

1-3-2b With the rewritten bat rules, there is no longer a requirement that any part other than the barrel be smooth and cylindrical. Therefore, bats with holes or edges in the taper area are legal.

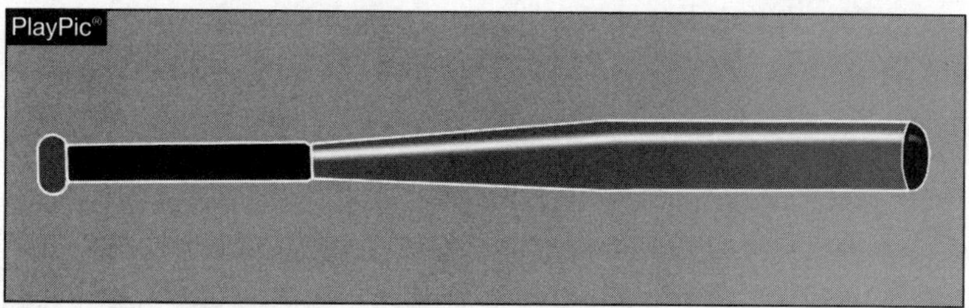

1-3-2c Non-wood bats must have a safety grip made of cork, tape (no smooth, plastic tape) or commercially manufactured composition material. The grip must extend a minimum of 10 inches, but not more than 18 inches, from the base of the knob. Slippery tape or similar material shall be prohibited. Resin, pine tar or any drying agent to enhance the hold are permitted only on the grip. Molded grips are illegal.

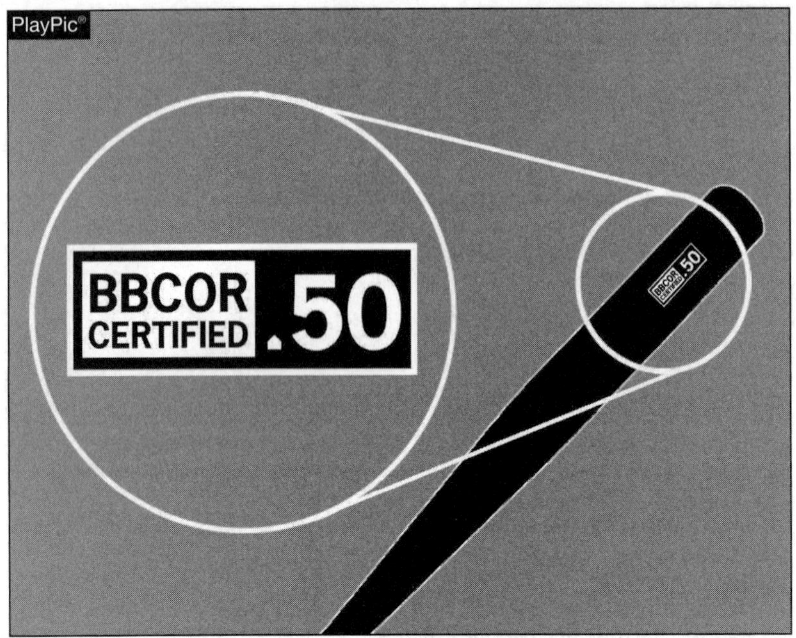

1-3-2d All non-wood bats must meet the Batted Ball Coefficient of Restitution (BBCOR) standard. Bats meeting that standard must be marked as shown above.

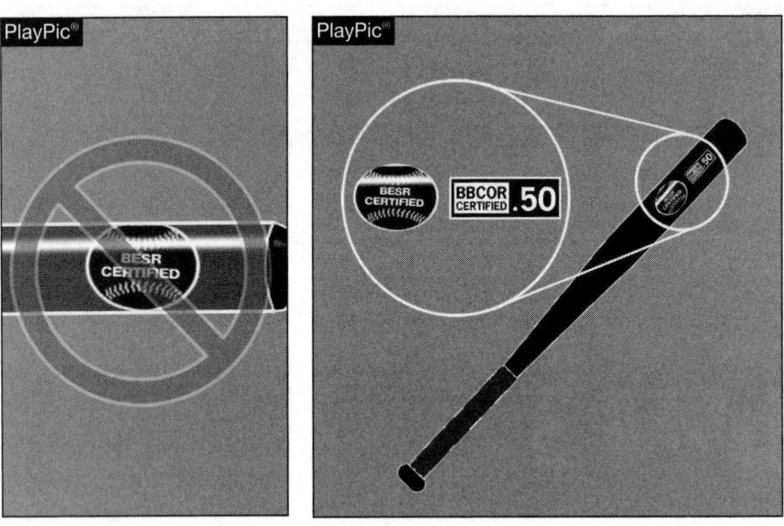

1-3-2d Bats marked with the BESR certification are not legal. A bat can be marked with both BBCOR and BESR certification and will be compliant.

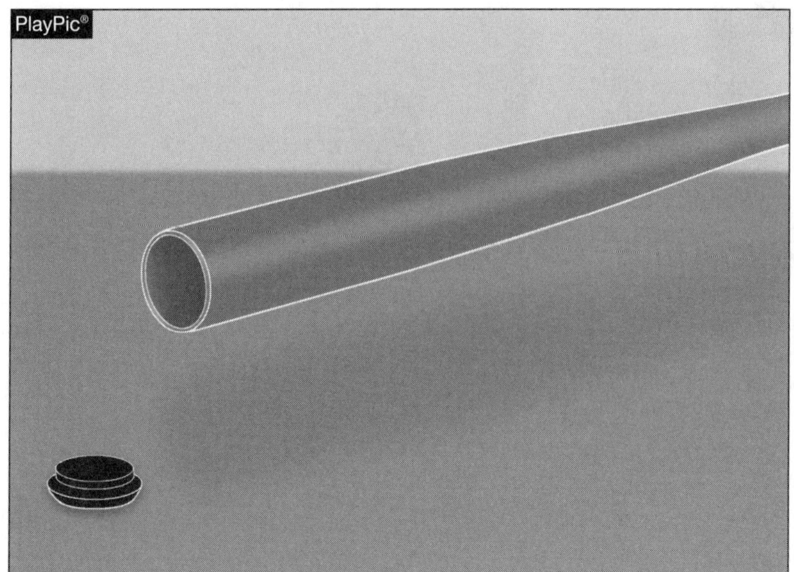

1-3-2 Note The altering of non-wood bats continues to be an important issue in high school baseball. It is the responsibility of players and coaches to ensure that bats are not altered.

1-3-2 Note The NFHS has been advised that certain manufacturers consider alteration, modification and "doctoring" of their bats to be unlawful and subject to civil and, under certain circumstances, criminal action.

1-3-4 Only bats and devices designed to remain part of the bat, such as weighted bats, batting donuts, and wind-resistant devices, may be used for loosening up (including weighted bats for this purpose) at any location. The player in PlayPic 1 is warming up legally, while the player in PlayPic 2, who is using a sledgehammer, is not in compliance with the rules.

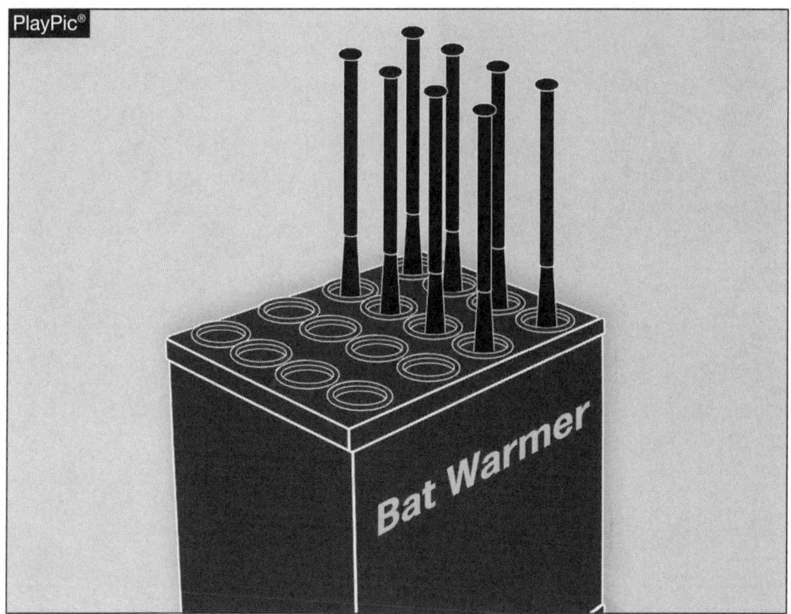

1-3-5 Any device used to control the temperature of a bat — whether to heat or cool it — is illegal.

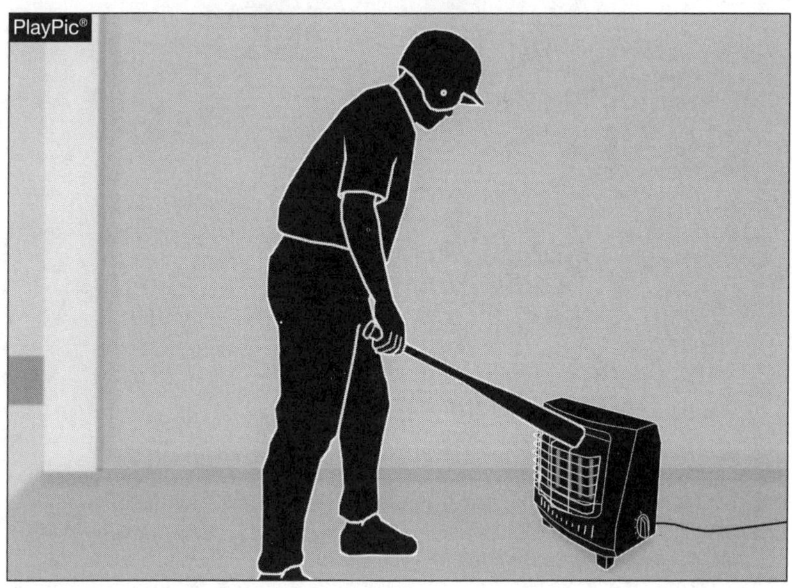

1-3-5 Along with the use of commercial warming devices, it is also illegal to control the temperature of a bat by intentionally holding next to a heater.

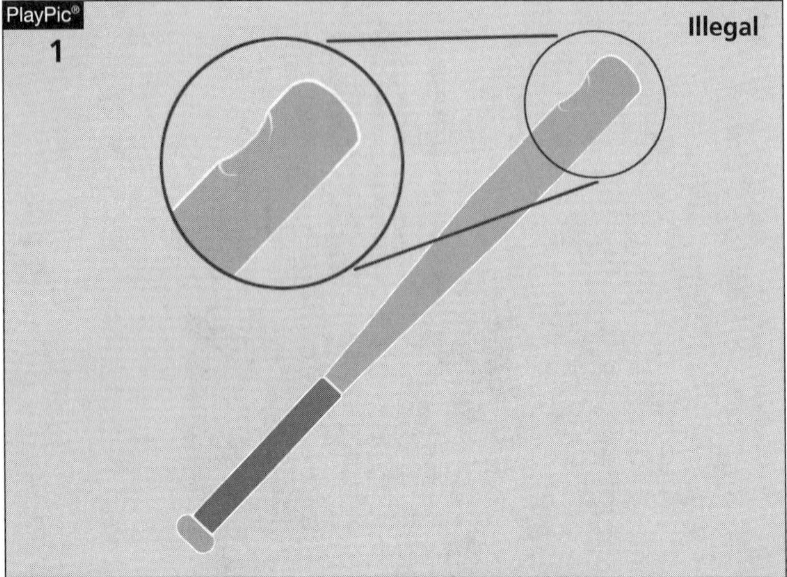

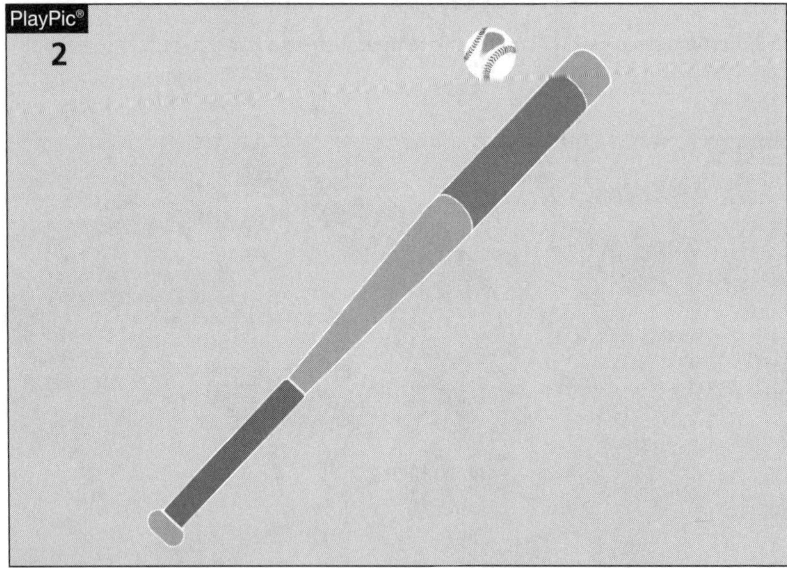

1-3-5 If a bat is broken, cracked or dented, it shall be removed without penalty (PlayPic 1). A bat that continually discolors the ball may be removed from the game with no penalty at the discretion of the umpire (PlayPic 2). Players who attempt to use such bats after they have been removed are then subject to the penalties for using an illegal bat. A player discovered using an illegal bat is out and no runners may advance because of a batter's actions with such a bat.

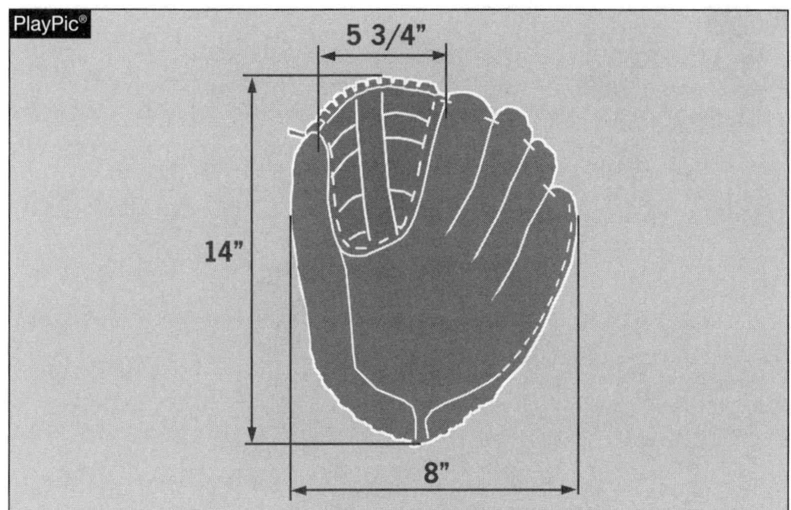

1-3-6 In high school baseball, a glove and a mitt are the same thing. The glove/mitt worn by all fielders other than the catcher shall conform to the following maximum specifications:

a. Height (measured from the bottom edge or heel straight up across the center of the palm to a line even with the highest point of the glove/mitt): 14 inches.

b. Width of palm (measured from the bottom edge of the webbing farthest from the thumb in a horizontal line to the outside of the little finger edge of the glove/mitt): 8 inches.

c. Webbing (measured across the top end or along any line parallel to the top): 5 3/4 inches.

A catcher's glove/mitt may be any size.

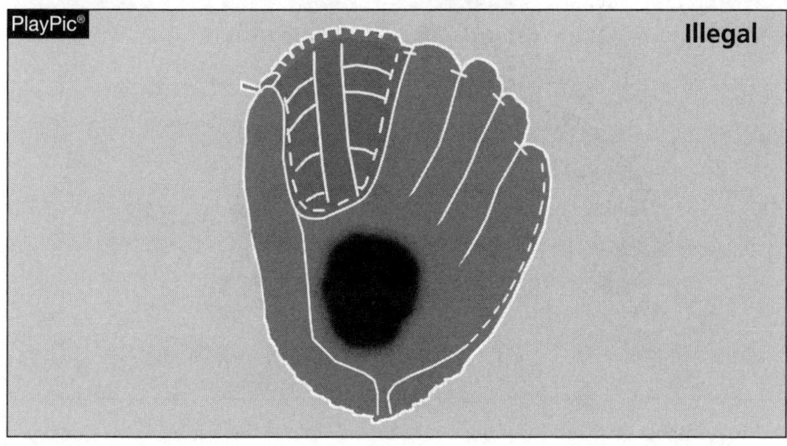

1-3-6 The glove shown here is illegal because it has been altered to create an adhesive, sticky, and/or tacky surface. Gloves/mitts may be softened with conditioner, provided it does not create a sticky, tacky or otherwise adhesive surface.

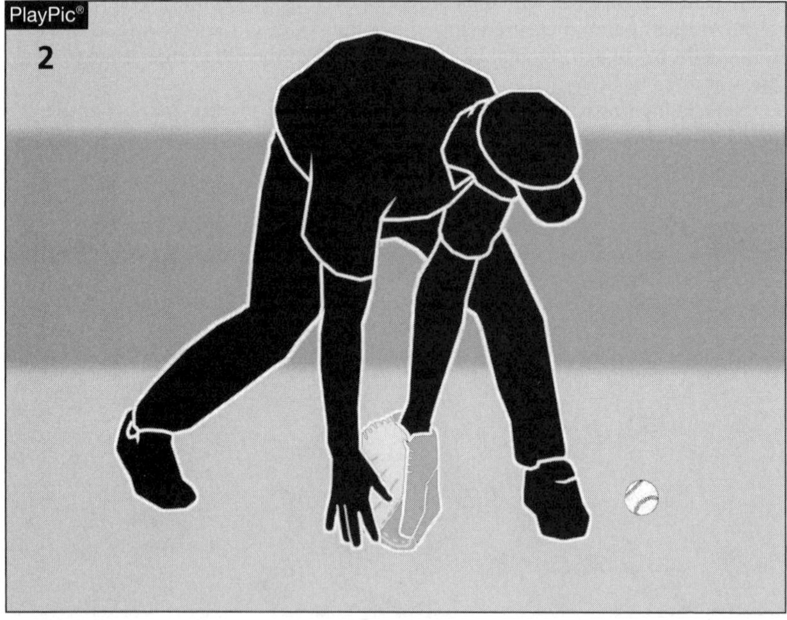

1-3-6 A pitcher may not wear a glove that contains white or gray. If the glove is discovered while he is pitching (PlayPic 1) or fielding (PlayPic 2), the penalty is that he must replace the illegal glove with a legal one.

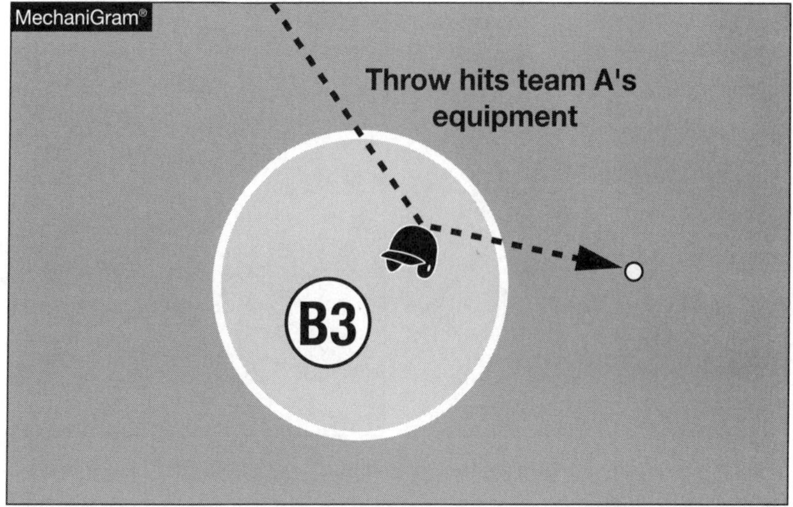

1-3-7 If a throw hits loose equipment, such as gloves, bats, helmets or catcher's gear, the umpires may call an out(s), award bases or return runners, based on their judgment and the circumstances concerning the play.

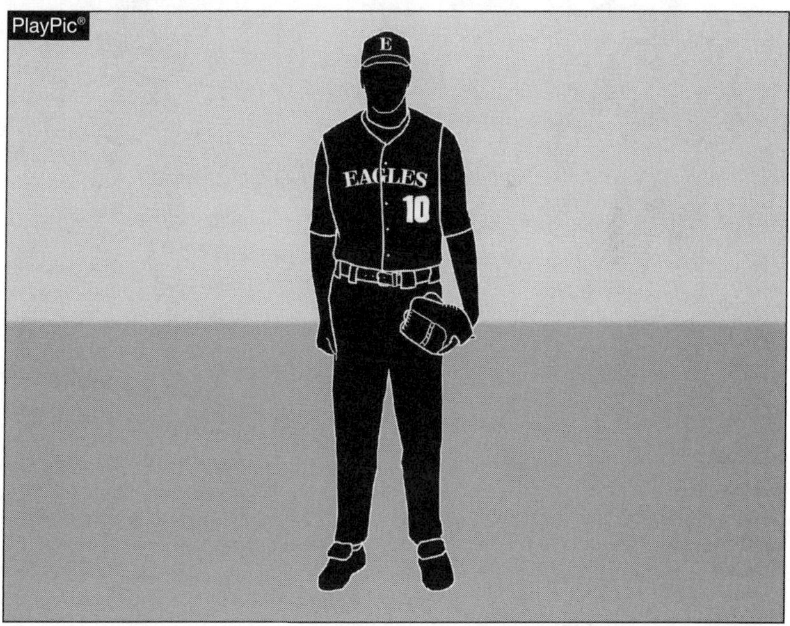

1-4-1 All members of the same team should wear uniforms of the same color and style. Caps and shoes are required equipment. When a player is required to wear a head protector, it replaces the cap as mandatory equipment.

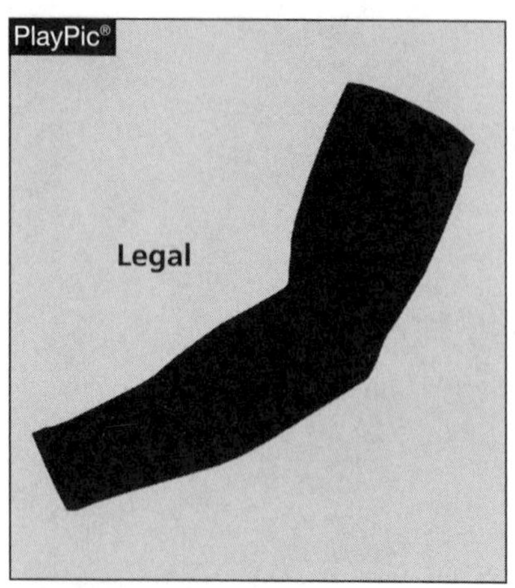

1-4-2 All compression sleeves must be solid black or solid dark color if the player is pitching.

1-4-2 When a team wears the vest style of jerseys, pitchers are allowed to wear white or gray undersleeves as long as the team is wearing all white/gray undersleeves. However, a pitcher's white/gray sleeves may not extend below the elbow.

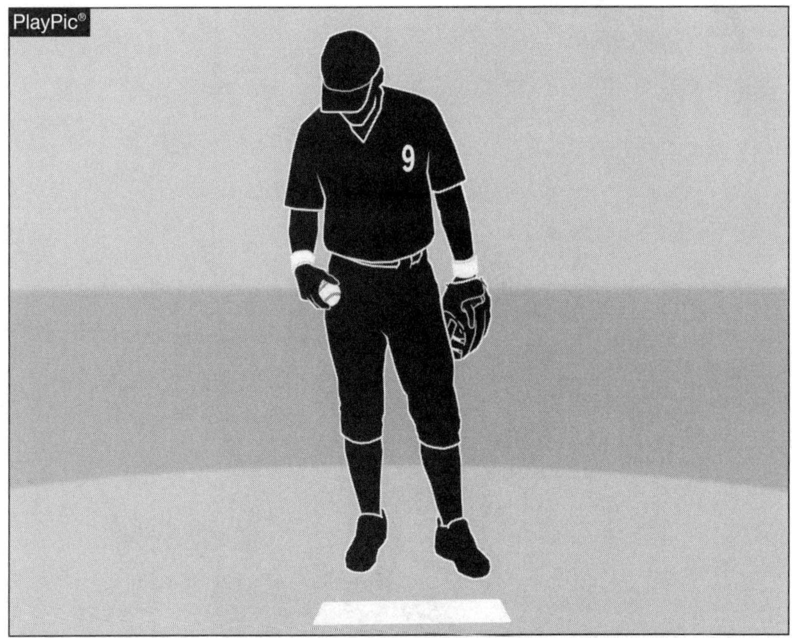

1-4-2 While individual players may have different sleeve lengths, sleeves of each individual player shall be approximately the same length and shall not be ragged, frayed or slit. The pitcher may not wear white or gray undersleeves if they are exposed. A pitcher also shall not wear any item on his hands, wrists or arms which may be distracting to the batter. The pitcher shown has a legal undershirt, but may not wear white wristbands.

1-4-3 Each of the players shown has a legal uniform number style on his jersey. Each number is plain and is a solid color that contrasts with the color of the shirt. Numbers shall be at least eight inches high, and no players on the same team shall wear identical numbers. A number may have a border of not more than one-quarter inch in width.

1-4-4 The uniform (including uniform pants, jersey, visible undergarments, socks, stockings, caps and headwear) may bear only a visible single manufacturer's logo. Each item of the uniform may also have a single American flag (no larger than 2 inches x 3 inches).

By state association adoption, to allow for special occasions, commemorative or memorial patches that are uniformly placed, not to exceed 4 square inches, may be worn on jerseys in an appropriate and dignified manner without compromising the integrity of the uniform. The player shown is wearing a legal uniform.

1-5-1 Coaches may, but are not required to, wear helmets while coaching the bases.

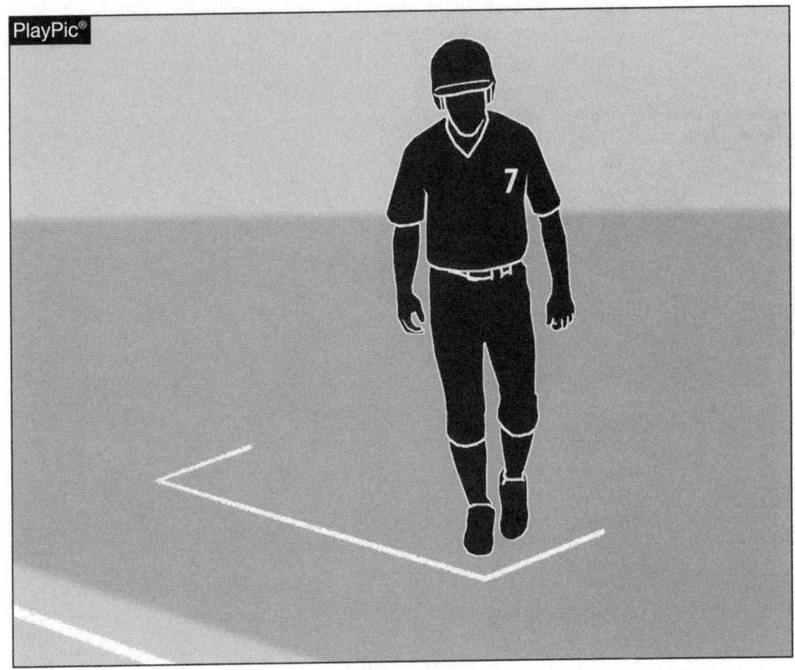

1-5-1 All non-adult personnel must wear a double ear flap, non-glare helmet that meets NOCSAE standards when coaching the bases.

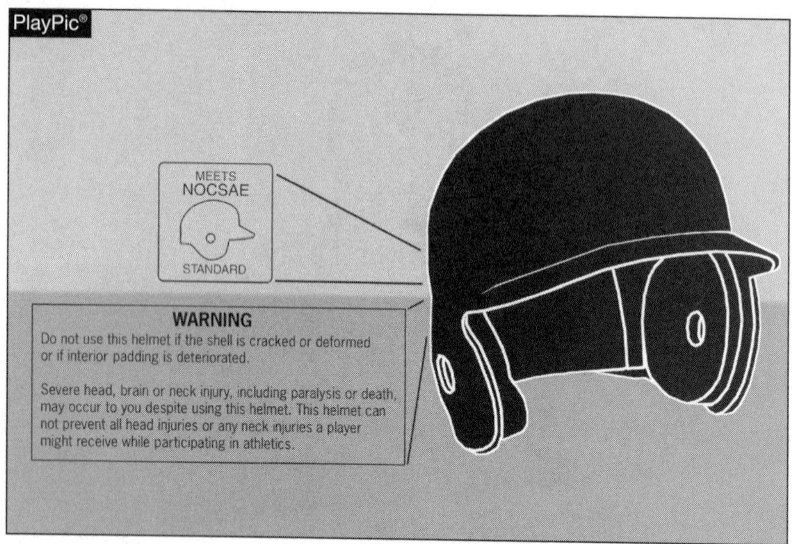

1-5-1 All batting helmets must meet the NOCSAE standard, must have extended ear flaps that cover both ears and temples and also display the NOCSAE stamp and the exterior warning statement. The warning statement may be affixed to the helmet in sticker form, or it may be embossed at the time of manufacture.

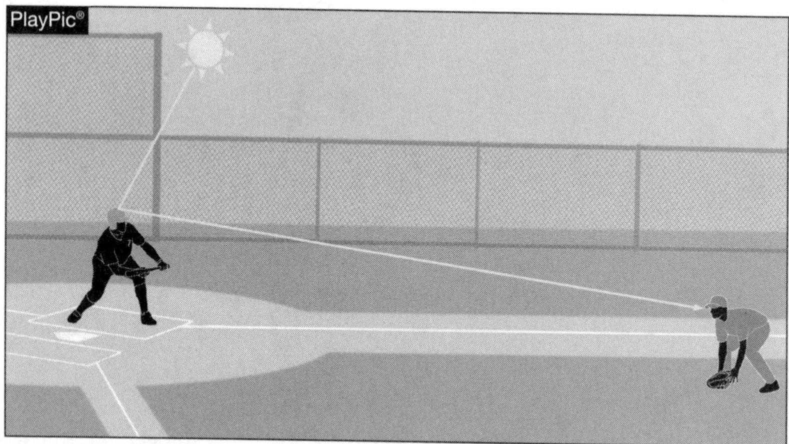

1-5-1 Batting helmets shall have a non-glare, non-mirror like surface and shall meet the NOCSAE standard at the time of manufacture.

1-5-1, 4-1-3b Even though this helmet met the NOCSAE standard at the time of manufacture, the crack makes the helmet illegal. The batter must replace the helmet immediately.

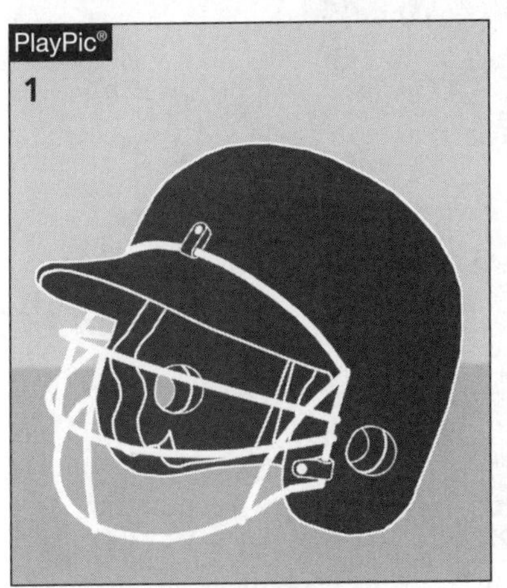

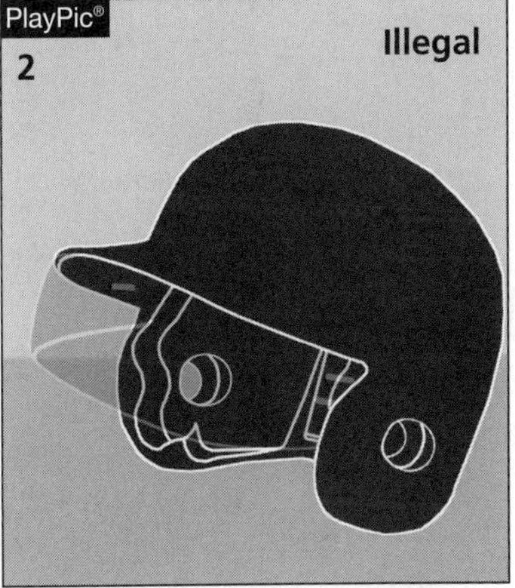

1-5-2 Face masks (PlayPic 1) may be attached to batting helmets at the time of manufacture. Such guards specifically designed for a particular helmet model may be attached after manufacture. All face mask/guards shall meet the NOCSAE standard. Shields (PlayPic 2) are not approved for use on batting helmets.

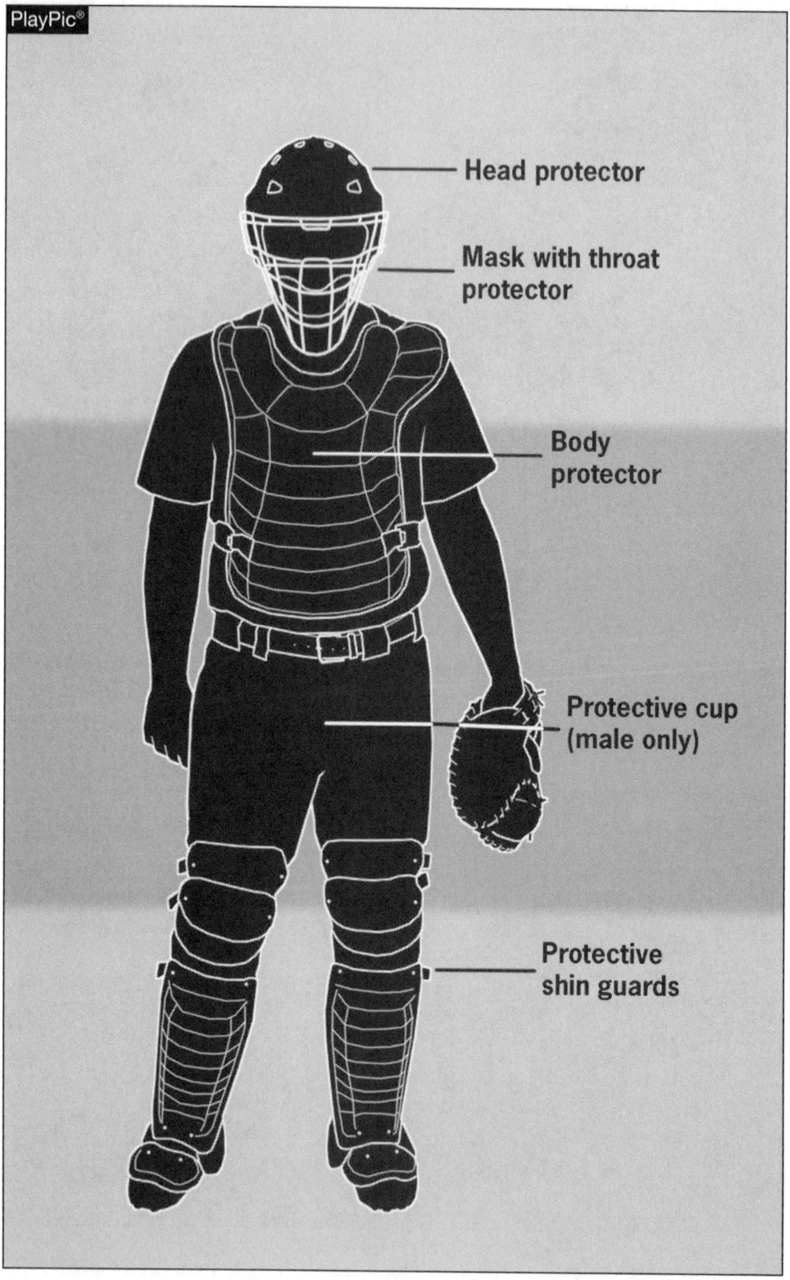

PlayPic®

Head protector

Mask with throat protector

Body protector

Protective cup (male only)

Protective shin guards

1-5-3 The catcher shall wear a head protector, a mask with a throat protector, body/chest protector that meets the NOCSAE standard (effective Jan. 1, 2020) and baseball protective shin guards. Male catchers shall also wear a protective cup.

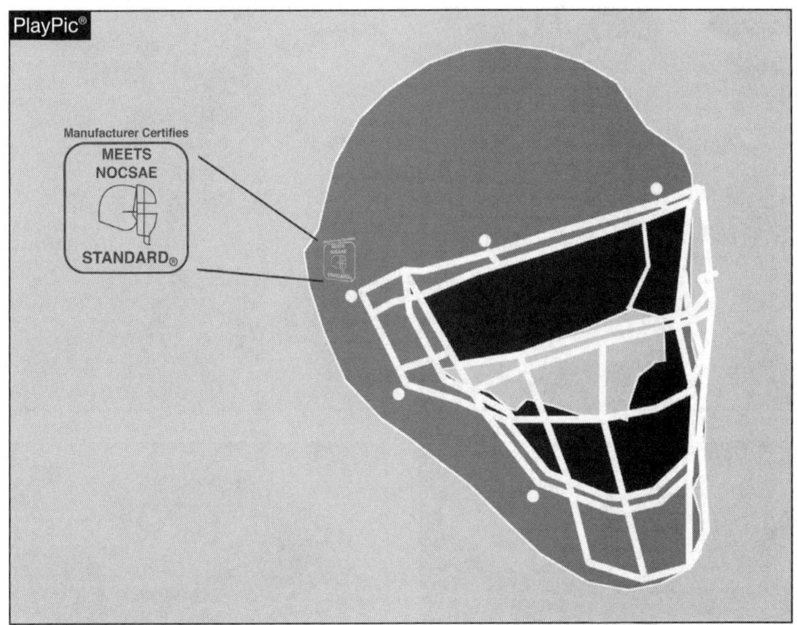

1-5-4 To be legal, a catcher's helmet and mask combination shall meet the NOCSAE standard, have full ear protection and have a throat protector that adequately covers the throat. The commercially manufactured catcher's head, face and throat protection may be a one-piece or multi-piece design.

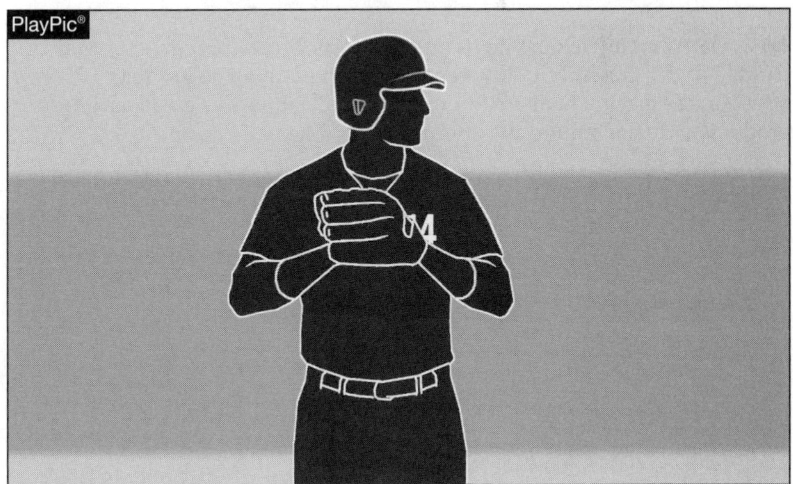

1-5-5 Defensive players are permitted to wear face/head protection in the field, as long as it has a non-glare surface.

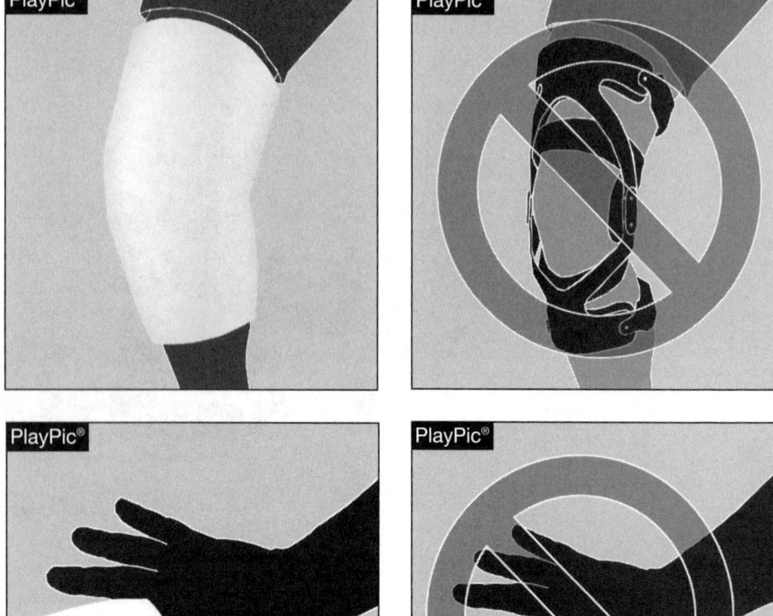

1-5-8 Hard and unyielding items (guards, casts, braces, splints, etc.) must be padded with a closed-cell, slow-recovery foam padding no less than 1/2-inch thick. Braces that are unaltered from the manufacturer's original design/production do not require any additional padding.

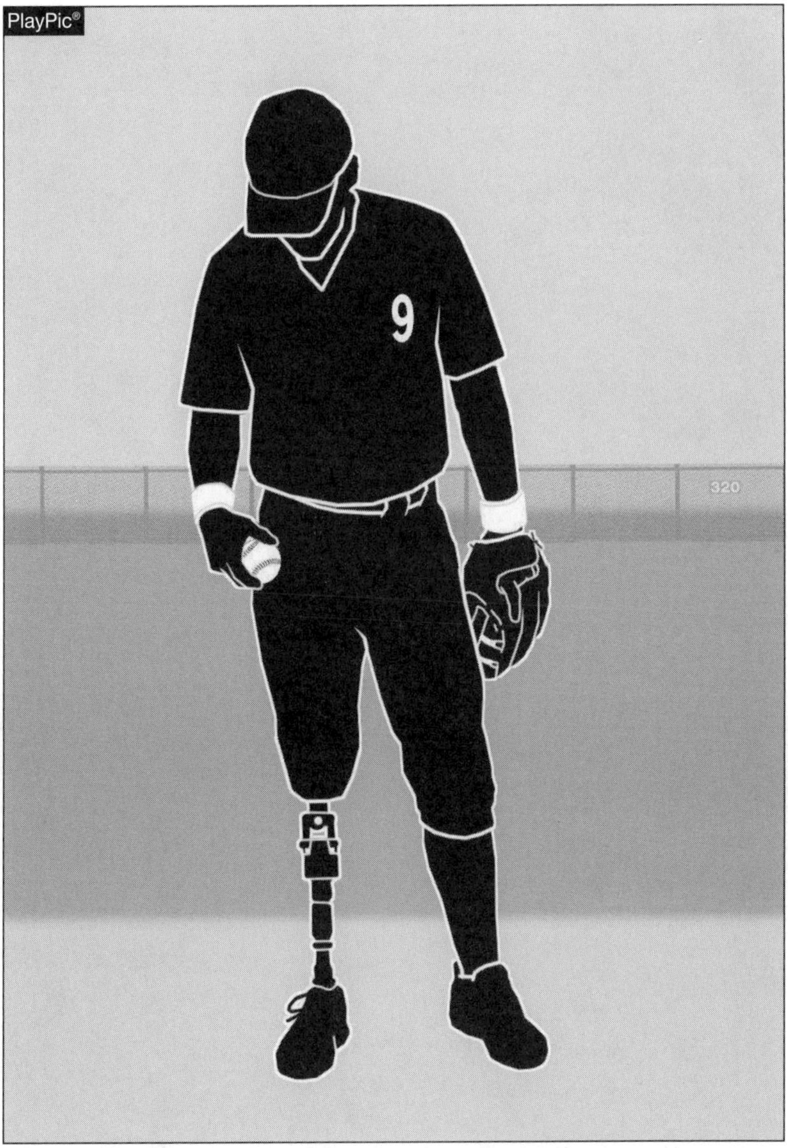

1-5-8 Each state association may, in keeping with applicable laws, authorize exceptions to NFHS playing rules to provide reasonable accommodations to individual participants with disabilities and/or special needs, as well as those individuals with unique and extenuating circumstances.

Part 3
Rule 2

Definitions

The basis for understanding any book is knowing and understanding the terms that are used in the book. It is imperative that instead of overlooking or browsing through this section of the rule book, that umpires and coaches fully comprehend all of the terms used to explain the rules. For example:

- A batted or thrown ball is in flight until it has touched the ground or some object other than a fielder.
- A batter-runner is a player who has finished a time at bat until he is put out or until playing action ends.
- A catch is the act of a fielder in getting secure possession in his hand or glove of a live ball in flight and firmly holding it, provided he does not use his cap, protector, mask, pocket or other part of his uniform to trap the ball.
- Obstruction is an act (intentional or unintentional, as well as physical or verbal) by a fielder, any member of the defensive team or its team personnel that hinders a runner or changes the pattern of play.
- A run is the score made by a runner who legally advances to and touches the plate.
- The strike zone is that space over the plate, the top of which is halfway between the batter's shoulders and the waistline, and the bottom being the knees, when he assumes his natural batting stance.

The argument can be made that the information contained in Rule 2 is the most important information in the rule book. Without a thorough understanding of this information, learning the other rules is difficult. The terms used in this section form the language of the game.

2-2-1 Runners must touch all bases when advancing, whether during a live or dead ball. When bases are awarded, it is the right to advance without a play being made that is awarded.

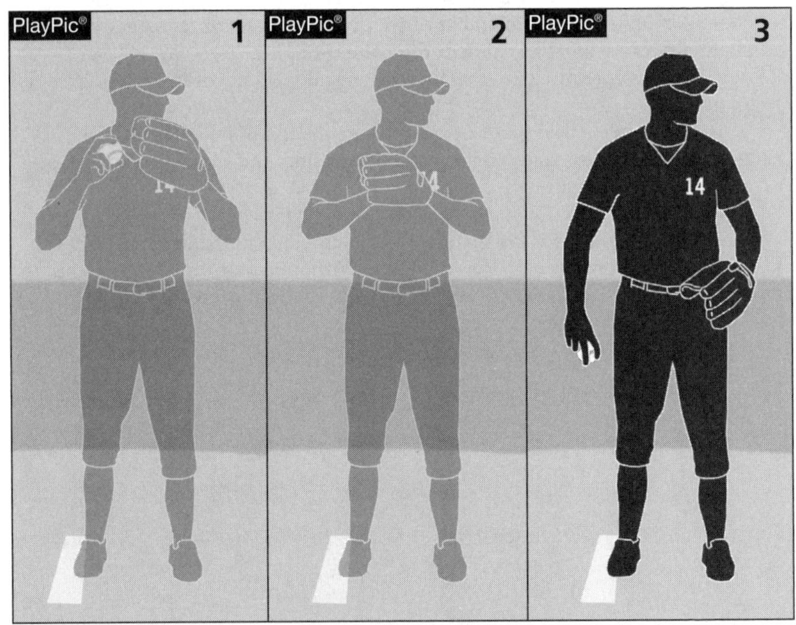

2-3 A balk is an illegal act committed by the pitcher with a runner or runners on base which entitles each runner to advance one base. Here, the pitcher balks by failing to come to a clear stop (Frame 2) as part of his pitching motion.

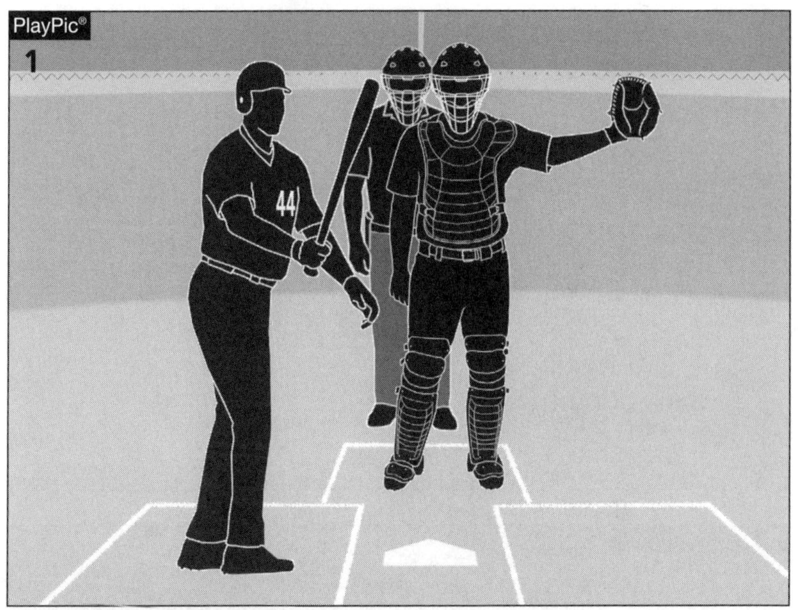

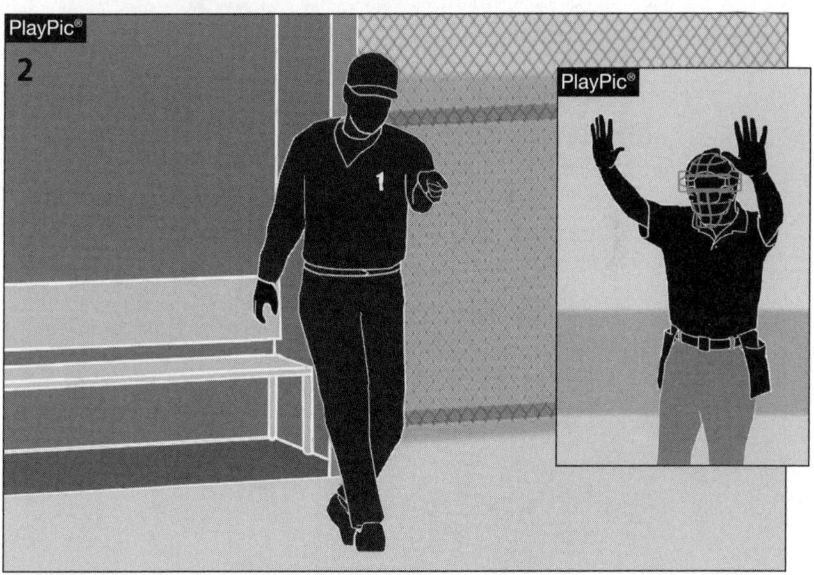

2-4-3 It is not necessary to throw four intentional balls (PlayPic 1) for an intentional walk. The defensive coach (PlayPic 2) or catcher may request the umpire to award the batter first base — before pitching to the batter or on any ball-and-strike count. The ball shall be declared dead before making the award.

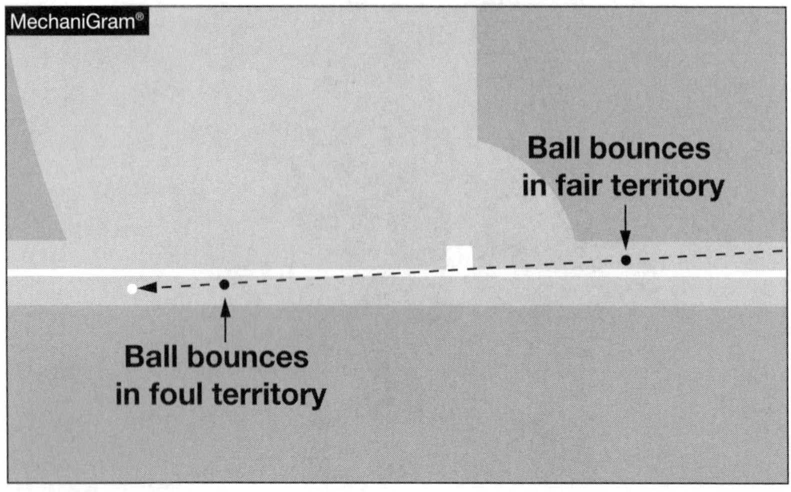

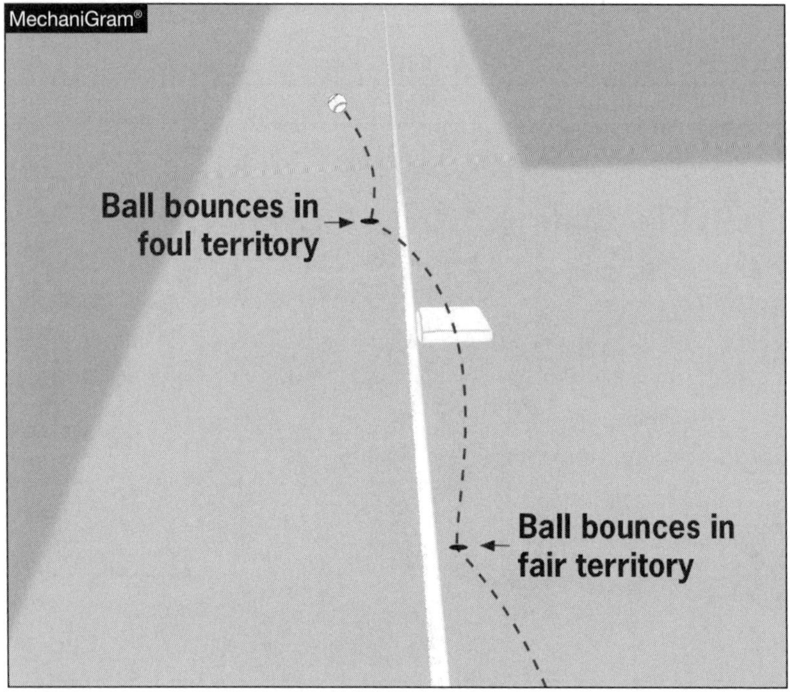

2-5-1 The same batted ball — shown from different angles in the MechaniGrams — bounced first in fair territory then went over third base. As a result, it is a fair batted ball.

2-8 A bunt is a batted ball in which the batter does not swing to hit the ball, but holds the bat in the path of the ball to tap it slowly to the infield. To be charged with a strike, a batter must have offered at the ball, not just held it out over the plate. The batter is out if he bunts the ball foul with two strikes (7-4-1e).

2-9-1 The fielder must demonstrate complete control of the ball and that his release is voluntary and intentional in order for there to be a catch. Until this fielder releases the ball voluntarily and intentionally, the catch is not complete.

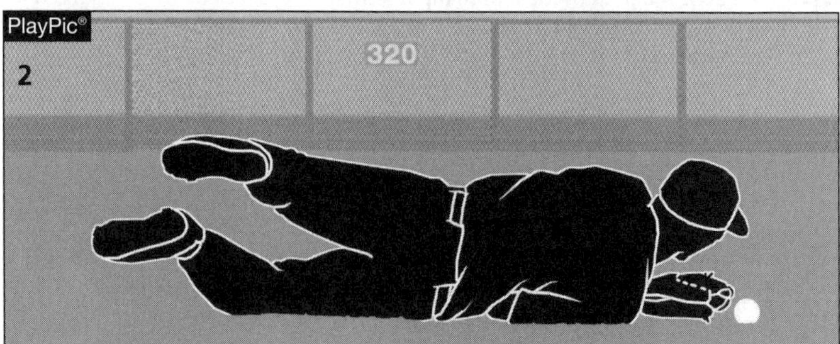

2-9-1 A catch of a fly ball is not completed until the continuing action of the catch is completed. The player in PlayPic1 initially caught the ball, but as can be seen in PlayPic 2, dropped it before securing possession and voluntarily and intentionally releasing the ball. That is not a catch.

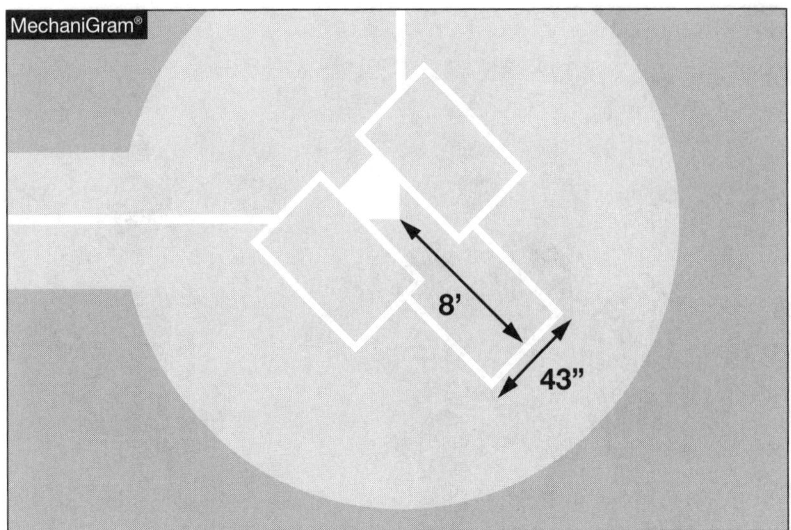

2-9-3 At the time of the pitch, the catcher must have both feet inside the catcher's box, which is 43 inches wide by 8 feet deep.

2-10-1 A charged conference is a meeting which involves the coach or his non-playing representative and a player or players of the team.

2-10-2 The pregame conference is a meeting involving the umpires, both head coaches and team captains (if available) near the plate. The meeting, which should begin approximately five minutes prior to the game, is held to exchange and check each team's lineup cards and to discuss ground rules. Umpires also shall ask the head coaches of the two opposing teams to verify the legality of their equipment and that all players are legally and properly equipped. Both teams shall remain in their dugout (bench) or bullpen area until this meeting has concluded.

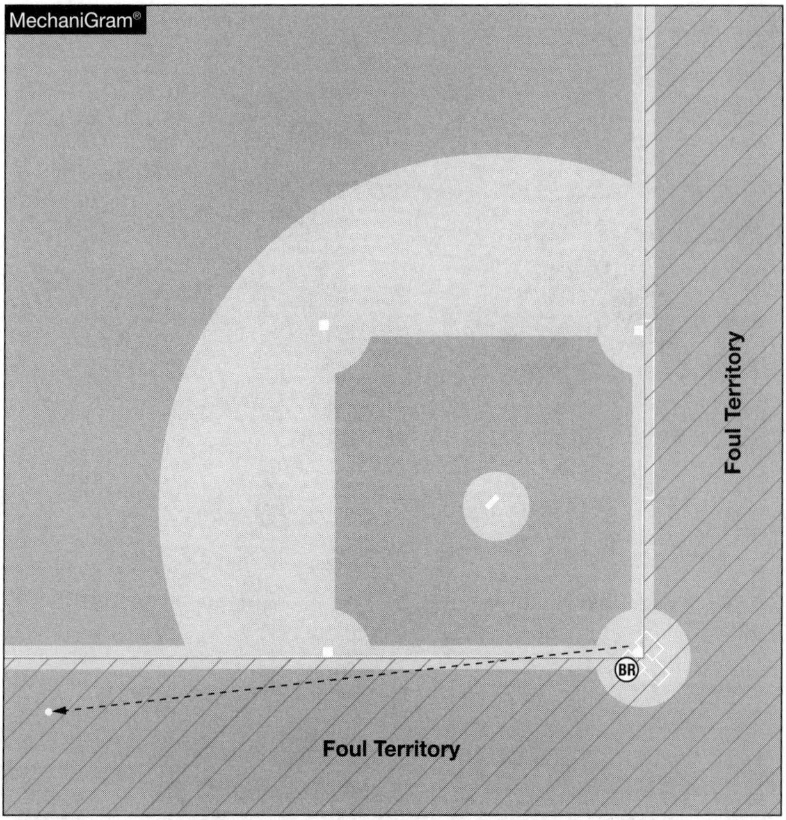

MechaniGram®

Foul Territory

BR

Foul Territory

2-16-1 A foul is a batted ball:

a. which settles on foul territory between home and first base or between home and third base; or

b. that bounds past first or third base on or over foul territory; or

c. that first falls on foul territory beyond first or third base; or

d. that, while on or over foul territory, touches the person of an umpire or a player or any object foreign to the natural ground; or

e. that touches the ground after inadvertently being declared foul by an umpire.

2-16-1f A batted ball that rebounds and hits the batter while he is still legally in the batter's box shall be called a foul ball.

2-16-1f Even though this batter has one foot completely outside the batter's box, he has one foot still in. Therefore, when the batted ball rebounds and hits him, it shall be called a foul ball.

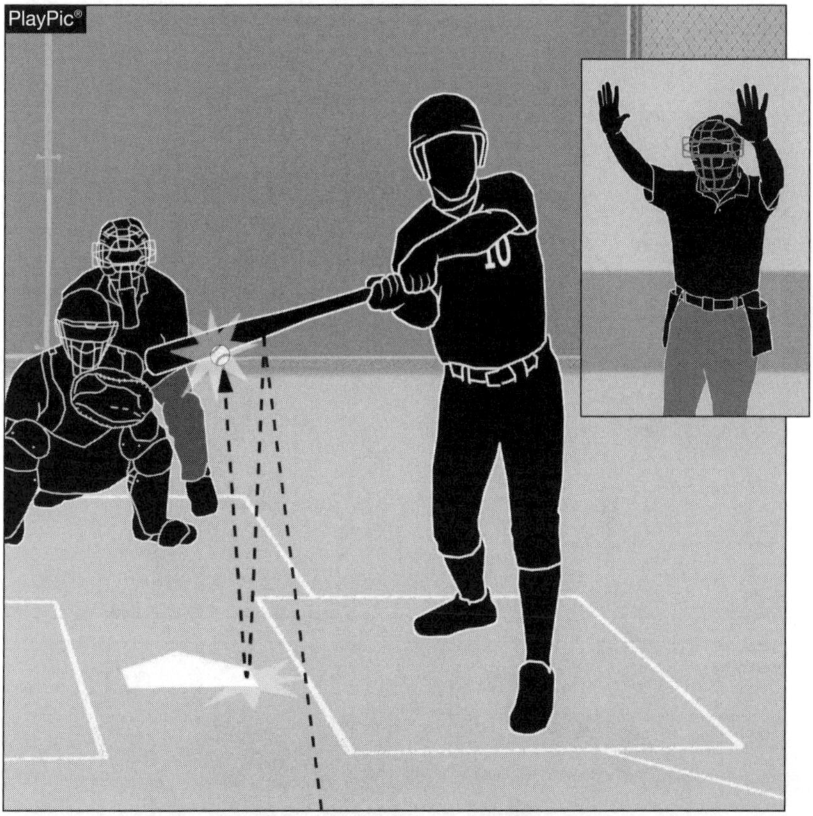

2-16-1g A batted ball that rebounds and hits the bat while the batter is still holding it while in the batter's box shall be called a foul ball.

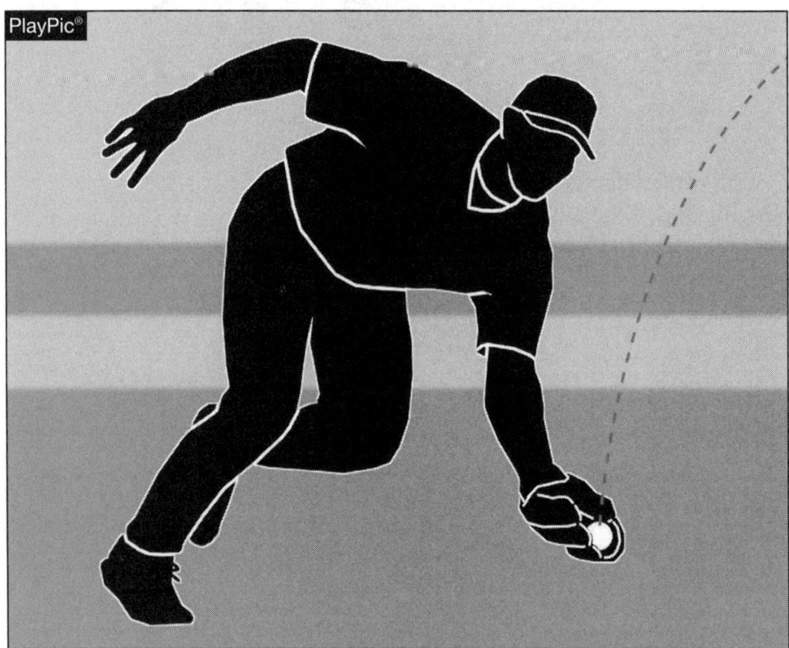

2-16-2 In order to meet the definition of a foul tip, the batted ball must go directly to the catcher's hand or mitt, but can only be caught by the catcher. If, after the batted ball goes directly to the catcher's hand or mitt, it is deflected and caught by another player, it is treated as an uncaught foul ball.

2-16-2 This bunt does not go directly to the catcher's glove, so the ball does not meet the definition of a foul tip. It has a perceptible arc and is a fly ball that can be caught by the catcher or another defensive player for an out.

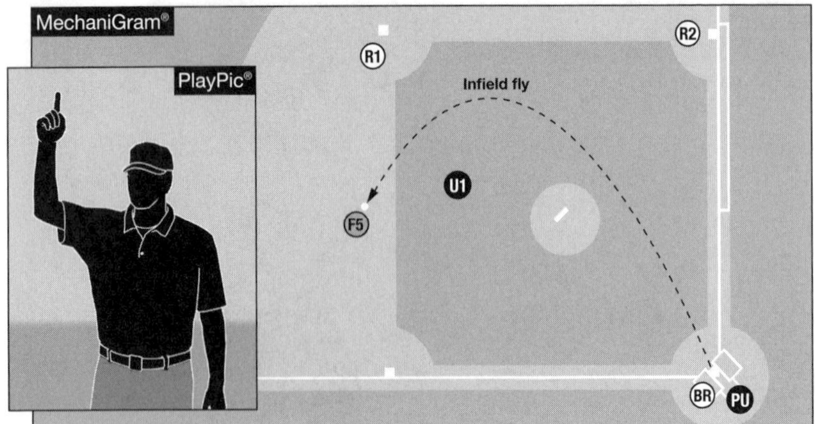

2-19 An infield fly is a fair fly (not including a line drive nor an attempted bunt) which can be caught by an infielder with ordinary effort, (rule does not preclude outfielders from being allowed to attempt to make the catch) and provided the hit is made before two are out and at a time when first and second bases or all bases are occupied.

When it seems apparent that a batted ball will be an infield fly, the umpire immediately announces it for the benefit of the runners. If the ball is near a baseline, the umpire shall declare, "Infield fly, if fair."

2-21-3 This fan is not guilty of spectator interference because he did not reach on to the field to prevent the fielder from making a play. A fielder is not protected when he reaches into the stands.

2-21-4 On his natural follow-through, the batter has made contact with the catcher. The ball is delayed-dead on follow-through interference and if F2 isn't able to throw out the runner attempting to steal, the runner must be returned to first base and the batter is out.

2-21-5 Before the time of the pitch, if the batter's practice swing makes contact with the catcher or his equipment, the umpire shall call an immediate dead ball. There is no penalty.

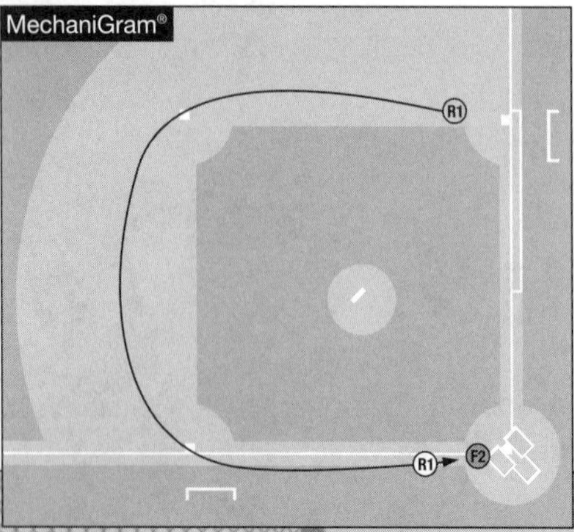

MechaniGram®

R1

R1

F2

PlayPic®

2-22-3 A fielder who does not have the ball may not deny a runner access to the base he is trying to reach. The runner has the right to reach a base without obstruction if a fielder does not have the ball.

2-22-3 Being in the act of catching the ball is not possession. The fielder is not allowed to deny the runner access to the base.

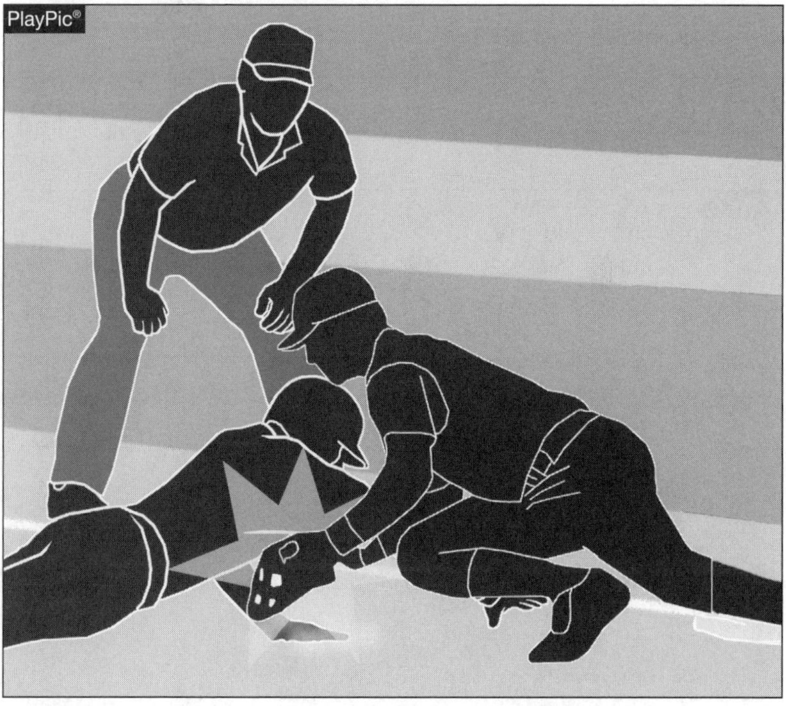

2-22-3 If the fielder has the ball, he is allowed to block the base and deny the runner access.

2-29-1 "Play" is the order given by the umpire when it is time for the game to begin, or to be resumed after having been suspended for any dead ball.

2-32-1 A legal slide can be either feet first or head first. If a runner slides feet first, at least one leg and buttock shall be on the ground.

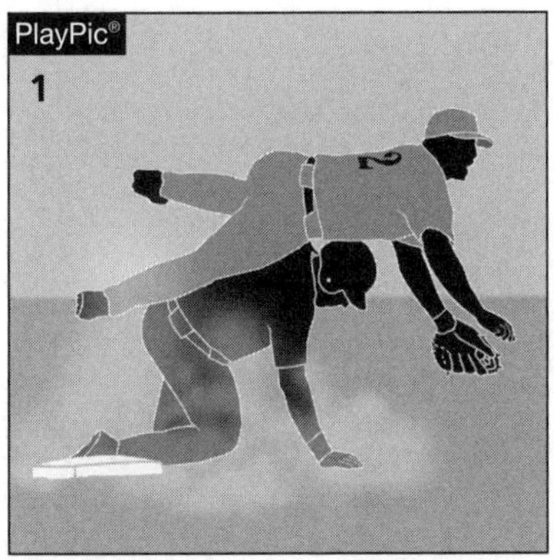

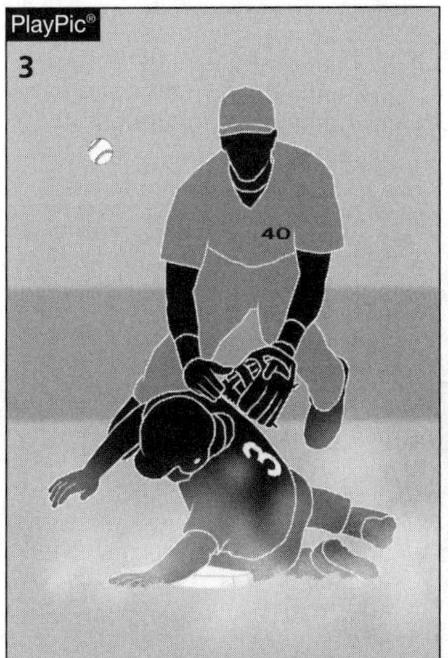

2-32-2 The four slides shown are all illegal. Runners may not pop-up into the fielder (PlayPic 1); have a leg raised higher than the fielder's knee (PlayPic 2); except at home plate, slide through or beyond the base (PlayPic 3); or slide away from a base in the direction of the fielder (PlayPic 4). At home plate, it is permissible for the slider's momentum to carry him through the plate in a straight line (baseline extended).

The runner is out when he illegally slides and affects the play. On a force play, the runner is also guilty of interference. The batter-runner is also declared out and all other runners must return to the base occupied at the time of the pitch. A runner may slide or run in a direction away from the fielder to avoid making contact or altering the play of the fielder (8-4-2b).

2-32-2c A runner may legally slide past home plate, even if he makes contact with a fielder or alters the play of the fielder, provided the slide meets all other provisions of the sliding rules and he does not initiate malicious contact.

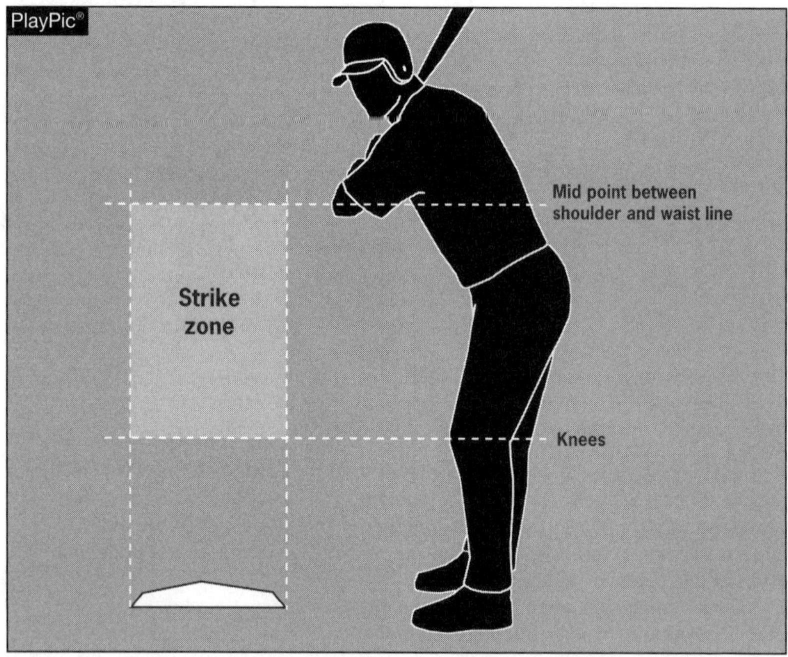

2-35 The strike zone is that space over the plate, the top of which is halfway between the batter's shoulders and the waistline, and the bottom being the knees, when he assumes his natural batting stance. If he crouches or leans over to make the shoulder line lower, the umpire determines height by what would be the batter's normal stance.

2-38 "Time" is the command of the umpire to suspend play. The ball becomes dead when it is given (5-2-1). Both umpires shown are signaling time. The umpire in PlayPic 1 is actually calling time, while the umpire in PlayPic 2 is giving the "Do Not Pitch" signal, which also creates a dead-ball situation.

Part 3
Rule 3

Substituting – Coaching – Bench and Field Conduct – Charged Conferences

So much of the "action" in baseball actually can happen when the ball is dead. All coaching moves — substituting, meetings with players and re-entering a player — occur during this time.

That rule also lists all of the actions that are prohibited by any coach, player, substitute, attendant or any other bench personnel and the penalties for when those violations occur.

The penalties range from a warning to ejection from the contest for acts such as carelessly throwing a bat to leaving the bench for a fight.

Requiring good sporting behavior is the essence of high school baseball. The result of the competition is important, but ensuring the participants enjoy the experience — both competitive and educational — is essential.

3-1-1 After the umpire has received the official lineup card prior to the game, the player listed as pitcher shall pitch until the first opposing batter has been put out or has advanced to first base. In any other case, a substitute may replace a player of his team when the ball is dead and time has been called.

3-1-1 When the coach has informed the umpire-in-chief of a change he wishes to make in the lineup, the substitution is official when the umpire-in-chief has made the change on his lineup card and informed the opposing team and official scorekeeper. A substitute does not have to be announced to become legal. An unannounced substitute becomes legal when he has entered the game, the ball has been made live and a runner takes the place of a runner he has replaced; a pitcher takes his place on the pitcher's plate; a fielder reaches the position usually occupied by the fielder he has replaced or a batter takes his place in the batter's box.

3-1-1 The runner shown is an illegal player. When discovered by an umpire or either team, that player shall be called out and restricted to the bench/dugout for the duration of the game. If a restricted player re-enters the game on offense, he shall be called out immediately and ejected.

3-1-1 The fielder shown is an illegal player. He shall be replaced immediately upon discovery by the umpire or either team and is restricted to the dugout. If an illegal defensive player is involved in a play, and the infraction is discovered by an umpire or either team prior to the first pitch to the next batter of either team, the team on offense has the option to let the play stand or to allow the batter to bat again. If a restricted player re-enters the game on defense, he shall be ejected.

3-1-2 If a pitcher is replaced while his team is on defense, the substitute pitcher shall pitch to the batter then at bat, or any substitute for that batter, until such batter is put out or reaches first base, or until a third out has been made. The umpire must deny any coach-defensive player conference that will violate the rule. If a pitcher is incapacitated or guilty of flagrant unsportsmanlike conduct, this rule is ignored.

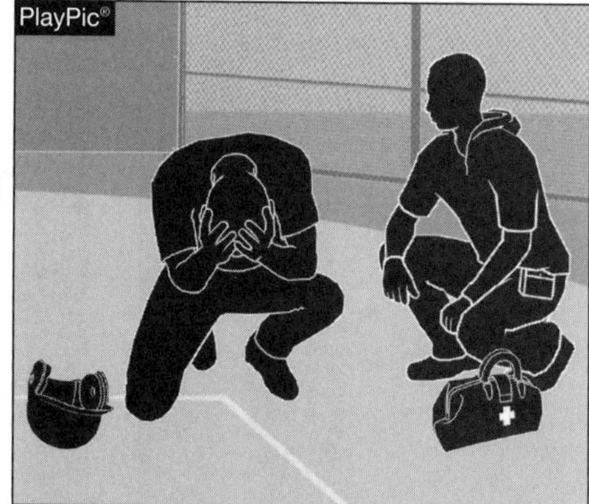

3-1-5 Any player who exhibits signs, symptoms or behaviors consistent with a concussion shall be immediately removed from the game and shall not return to play until cleared by an appropriate health-care professional. Possible signs or symptoms include loss of consciousness, headache, dizziness, confusion and balance problems.

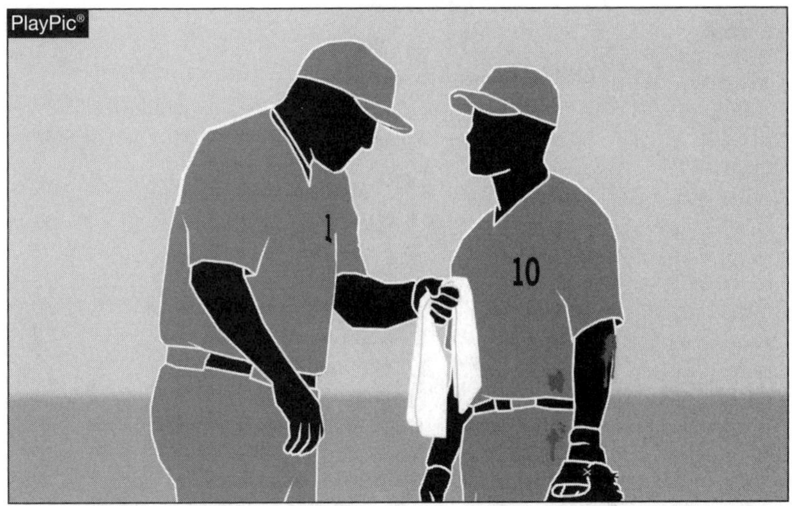

3-1-6 A player who is bleeding, has an open wound or has any amount of blood on his uniform shall not play until the bleeding has stopped, wound has been covered or uniform is cleaned or changed. The re-entry rule applies for starters who wish to return to the game.

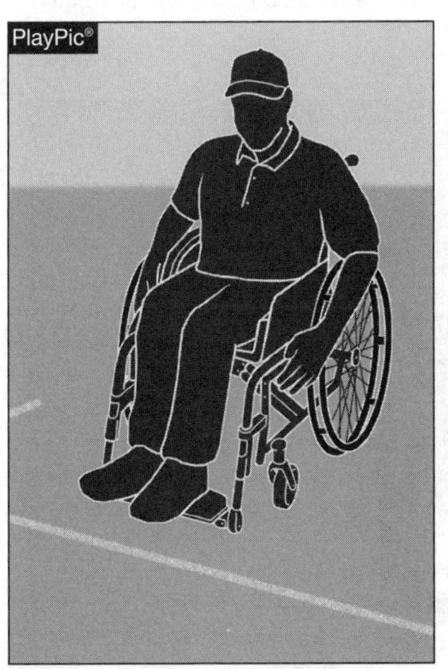

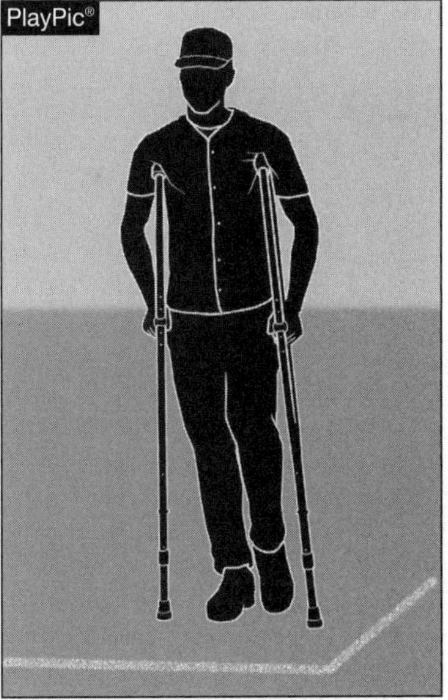

3-2-1 Wheelchairs, crutches and other mobility devices may be used by coaches while in a coaching box.

3-2-1 In order to occupy a coach's box while his team is at bat, a coach or player must be in the team's proper uniform. The coach pictured here is not legal because he is wearing a business suit. Any non-adult in the coaching box must wear a batting helmet.

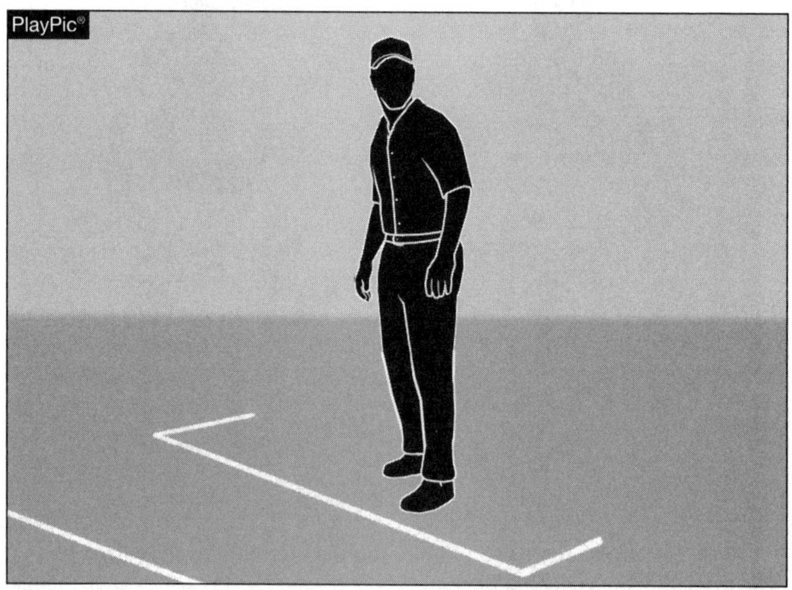

3-2-1 A coach may (but is not required) to occupy either coaching box. He is not required by rule to occupy the box.

3-2-2 Penalty and 8-4-2s If a runner is physically assisted by a coach, the runner is called out immediately and the ball remains live for any other runners to be put out.

3-2-3 The base coach must vacate the area if a fielder is attempting to make a play. When the base coach interferes, as shown here, the ball is dead immediately and the batter is out. All runners must return to the base occupied at the time of the pitch.

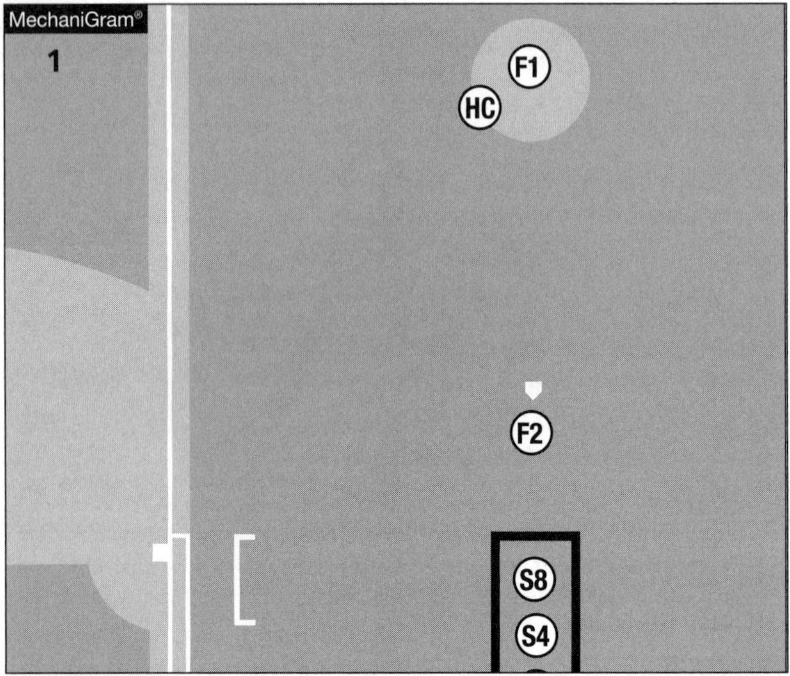

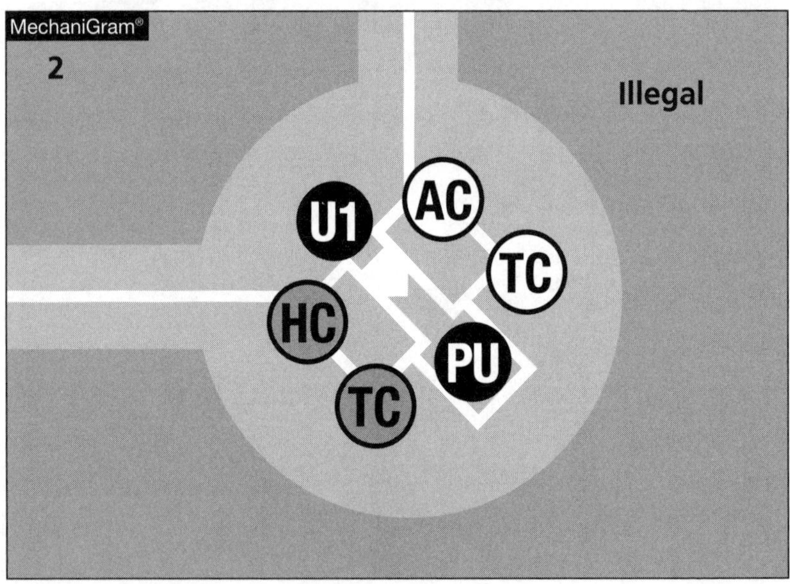

3-2-4 If available, the head coach must attend the plate meeting. A head coach can not be with his pitcher (MechaniGram 1) while sending the assistant coach and team captain (MechaniGram 2) to the plate meeting.

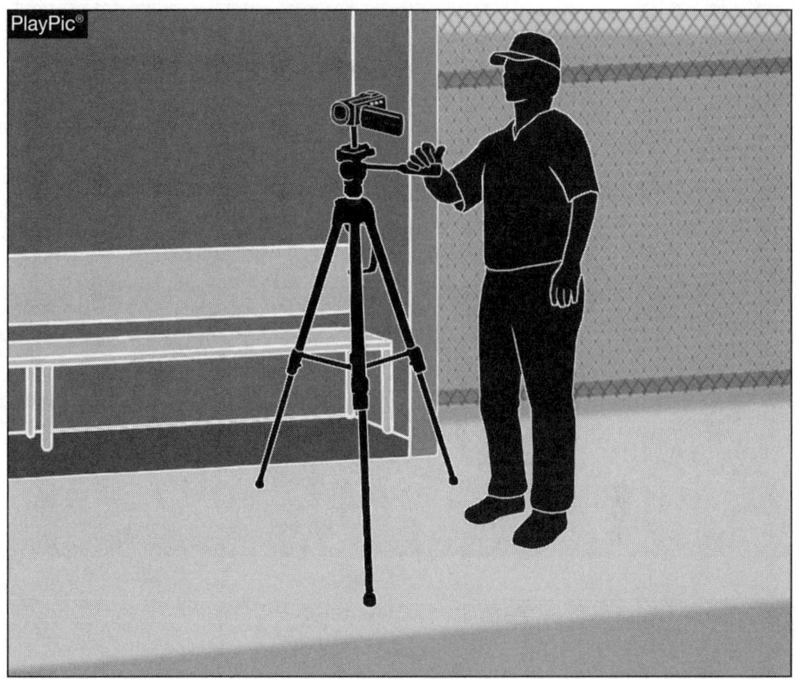

3-3-1 The rule that prohibited using video for coaching purposes during a game has been removed. Therefore, it is legal for a coach or player to use a camera, tablet or phone to record video during a game from the dugout.

3-3-1 Not only may teams record video during the game, but they may also watch it for coaching purposes.

PlayPic®

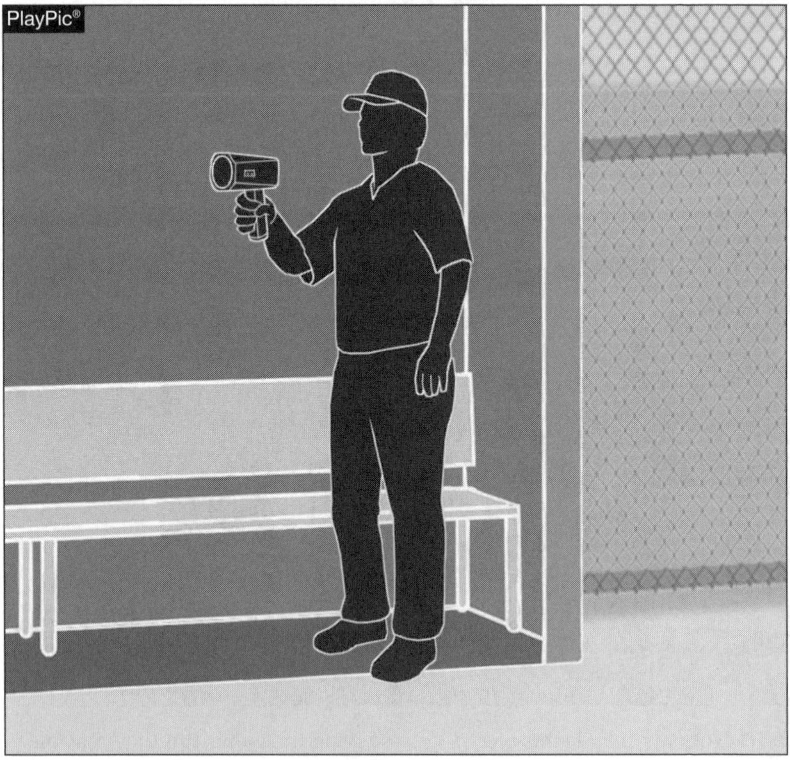

3-3-1 The use of radar guns is legal.

3-3-1, 10-1-5 A coach is not permitted to show a play to umpires, as umpires are not allowed to use video equipment during a game. If a coach persists, he can be warned and restricted to the dugout or ejected.

3-3-1 Penalty Umpires have access to a three-tier system for dealing with coaches' misconduct: verbal warning, written warning with restriction to the dugout and, finally, ejection.

3-3-1 Penalty If the umpire judges an offense to be minor, the umpire shall issue a verbal or written warning.

3-3-1 Penalty For any minor violation of Rule 3-3-1f, 1-5, (g-k), the offending coach will receive a written warning and will be restricted to the bench/dugout for the remainder of the game.

3-3-1 Penalty After the written warning and the coach is restricted to the bench/dugout, if the coach commits another offense, the umpire will eject the coach from the game.

3-3-1 Penalty If the umpire deems the offense to be major, such as, "physical contact, spitting, kicking of dirt or any other physical action directed toward an umpire," the umpire shall immediately eject the coach from the game.

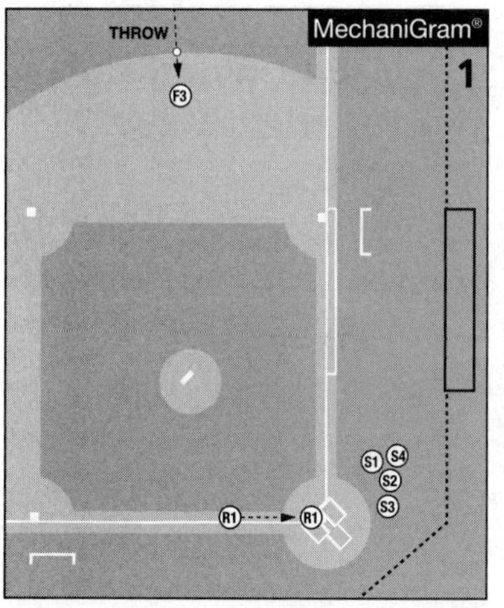

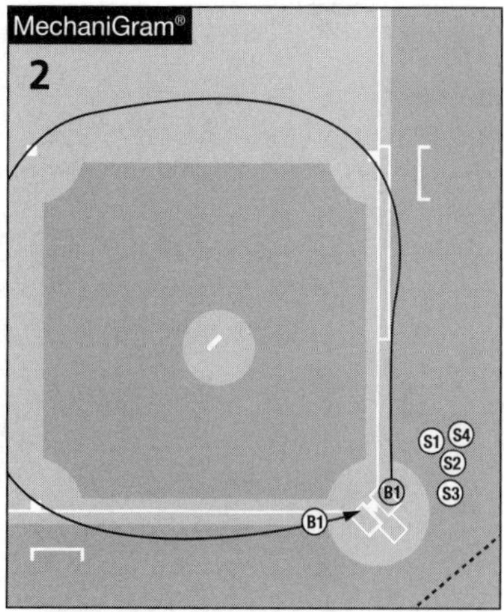

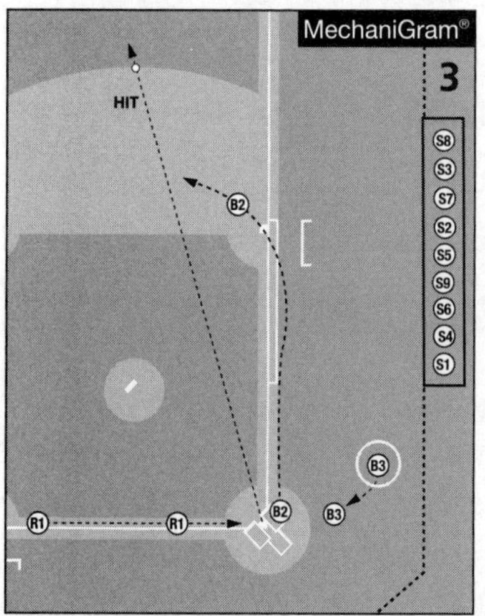

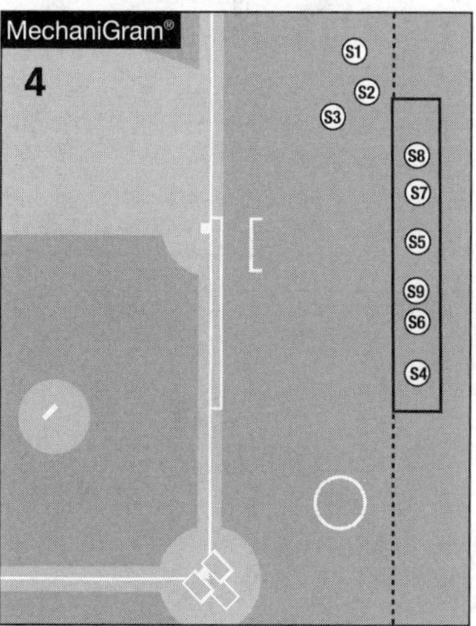

3-3-1a No offensive personnel — coach, player, substitute, attendant or other bench personnel — may leave the dugout during a live ball for an unauthorized purpose. At the end of playing action, the umpire shall issue a warning to the coach of the team involved and the next offender on that team shall be ejected. In MechaniGram 1, the offensive team is guilty of a violation since the ball is live and they are on the field. In MechaniGram 2, the offense is allowed to congratulate a player after hitting a home run. MechaniGram 3 shows the on-deck batter going to the the plate area to assist R1, which is legal. MechaniGram 4 shows S1 and S2 going to the bullpen to warmup with S3 going to protect them. That is legal.

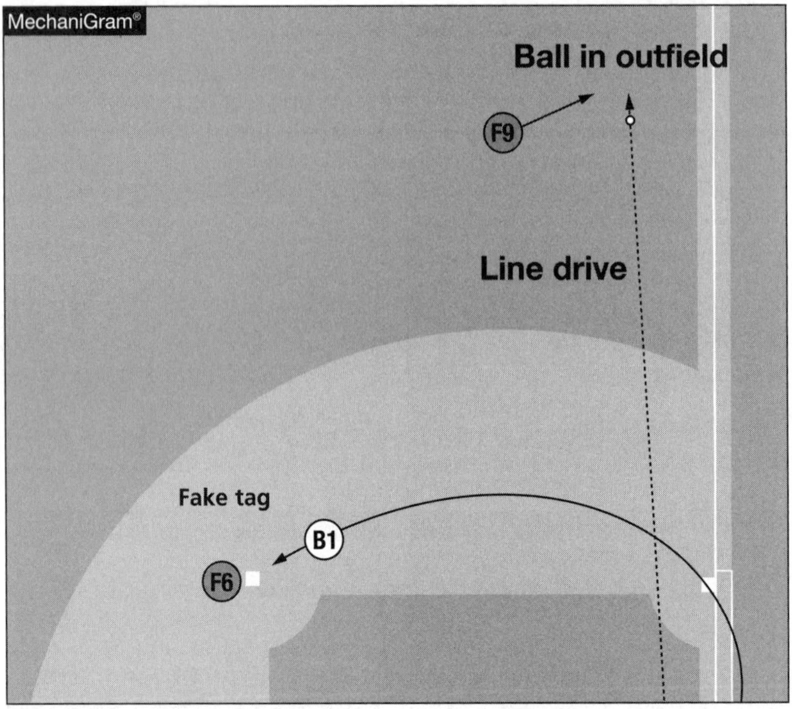
MechaniGram®
Ball in outfield
F9
Line drive
Fake tag
B1
F6

PlayPic®
Fake tag
30

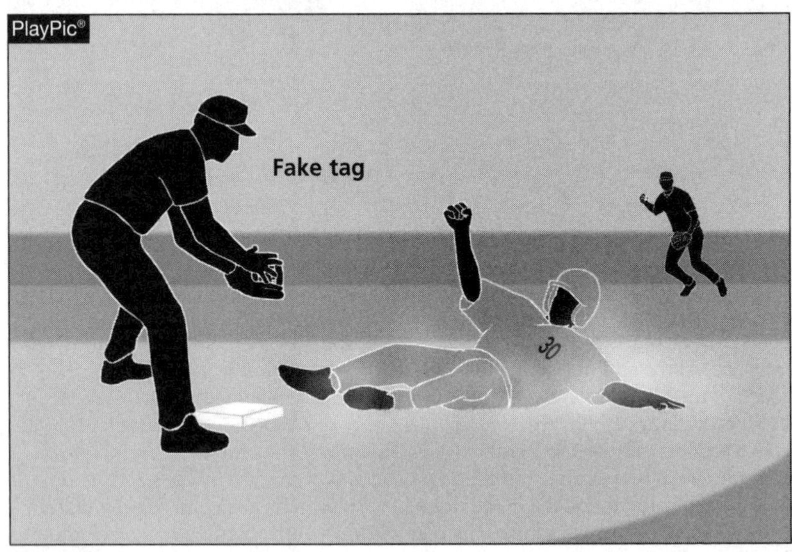

3-3-1b A player may not fake a tag without the ball. The defensive player is guilty of obstruction (8-3-2). Also, at the end of playing action, the umpire shall enforce the penalty for obstruction and issue a warning to the coach of the team involved. The next offender on that team shall be ejected.

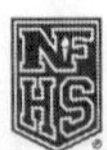

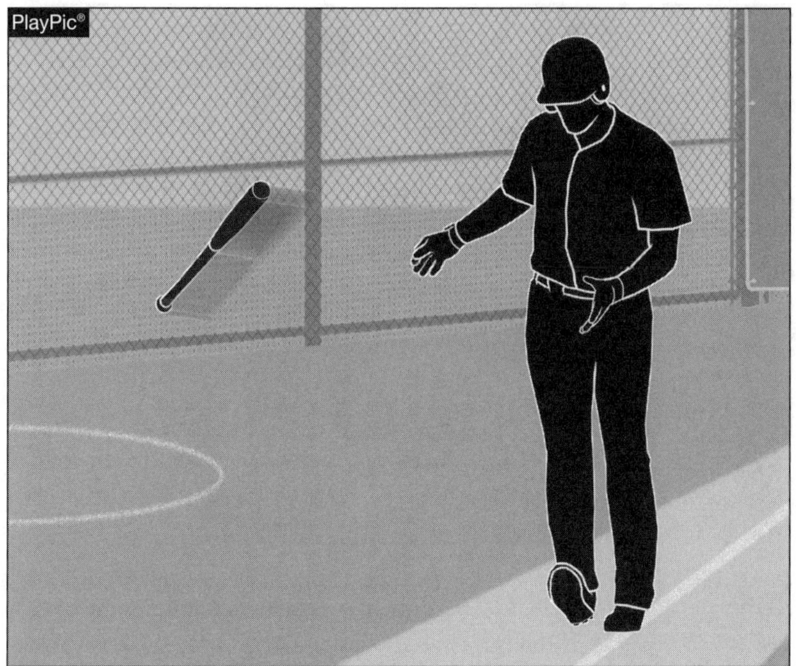

3-3-1c A player shall not carelessly throw a bat. At the end of playing action, the umpire shall issue a warning to the coach of the team involved and the next offender on that team shall be ejected.

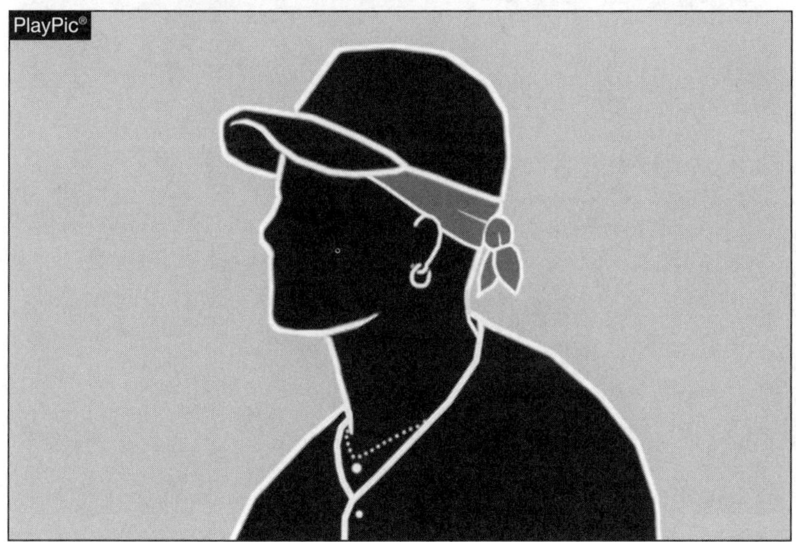

3-3-1d The player shown here may not participate in the game because he is wearing jewelry. A bandana may not be worn at anytime on the field.

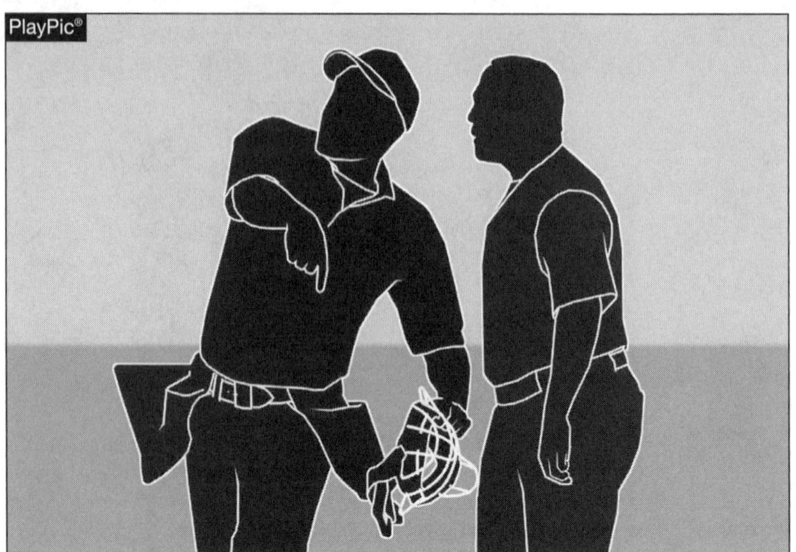

3-3-1f (1-5) Penalty For coaches who violate these acts, the umpire will restrict the coach to the bench/dugout for the remainder of the game or eject the coach from the game.

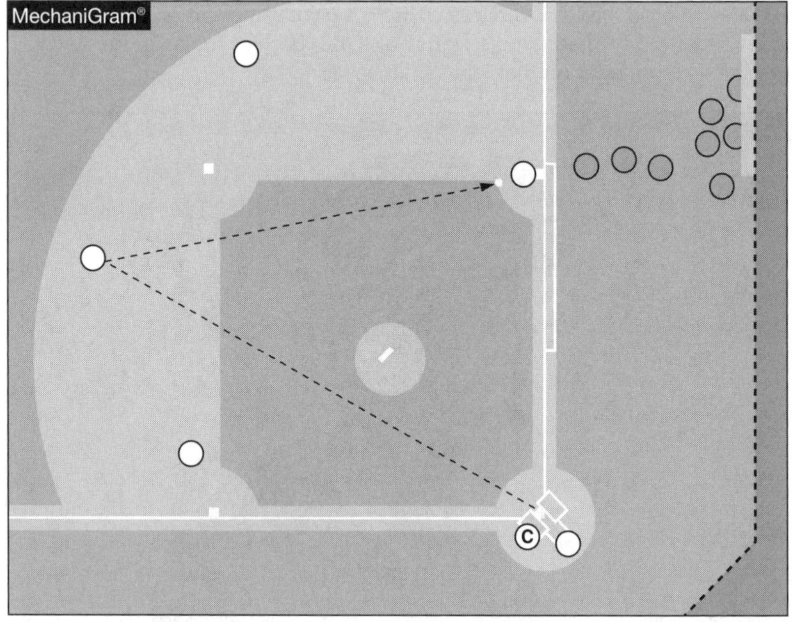

3-3-1f(5) While a team is taking its pregame warmup drills, no member of the other team — coach, player, substitute, attendant or other bench personnel — is allowed in live ball territory (excluding the bullpen area).

3-3-1f(6) Assistant coaches are not permitted to leave the dugout or the coaching box for the purposes of arguing with an umpire (PlayPic 1). The assistant coach is either restricted to the dugout or ejected and the head coach is restricted to the dugout. If an assistant coach has left the box for another purpose (for example, returning to the dugout in between innings), he may still be restricted or ejected for arguing with an umpire, but the head coach is not affected (PlayPic 2).

3-3-1f(7) Umpires are protected from altercations following a game. Umpires should report a coach's actions to the state association office. That office will determine appropriate punishment.

3-3-1g A player shall not enter the area behind the catcher while the opposing pitcher and catcher are in their positions, either to warm up (as shown) or for any other reason.

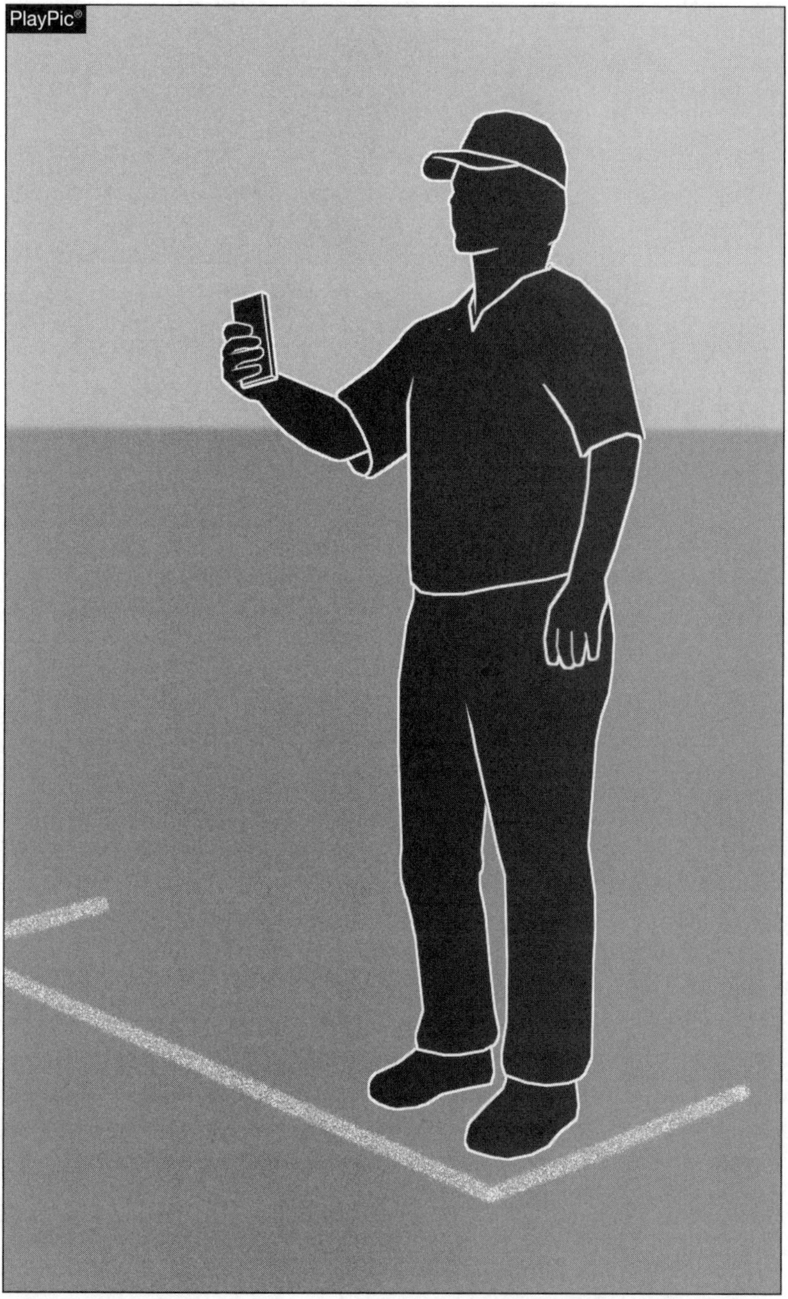

3-3-1h Although it is now legal to use video for coaching purposes during a game, a coach is not permitted to record while in the coaching box. A coach may only have a stopwatch, rule book (hard copy) and scorebook while coaching in the box.

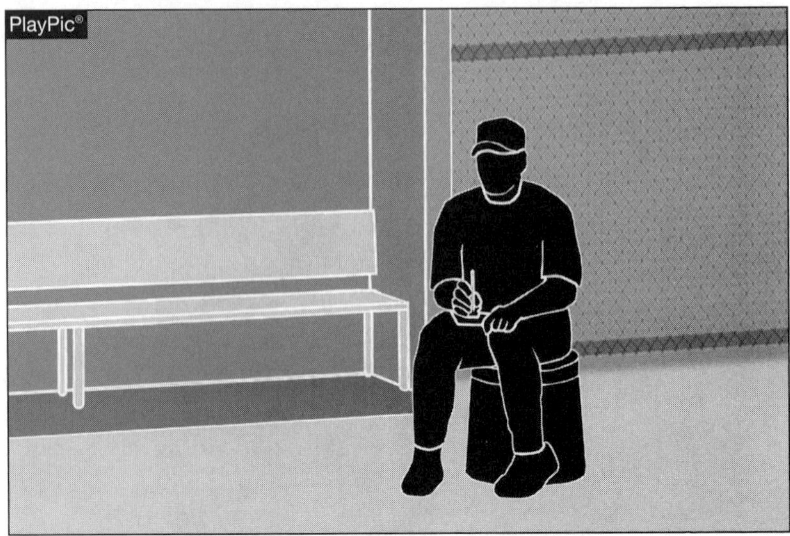

3-3-1i A coach is not allowed to sit outside the designated dugout (bench) or bullpen area. Coaches must be in the dugout or in the coaching box.

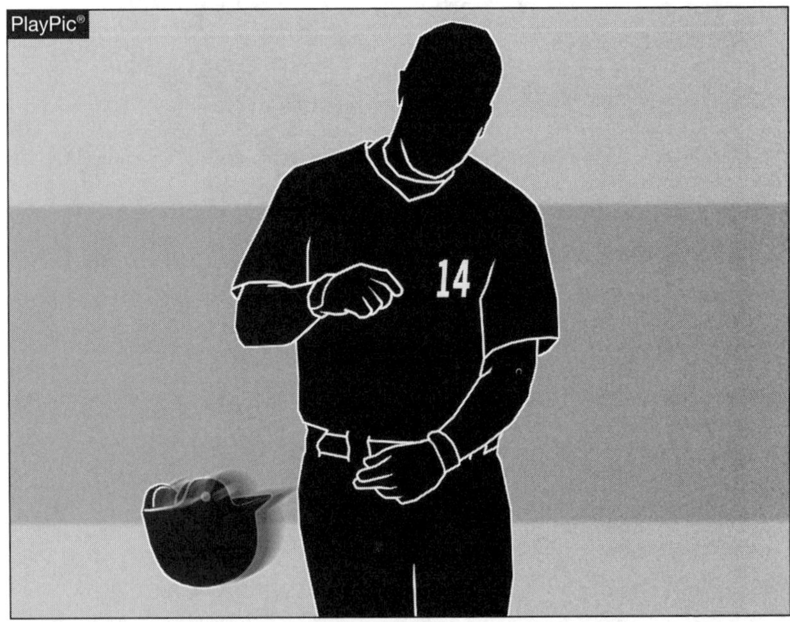

3-3-1l Deliberately throwing a bat or helmet is illegal and cause for immediate ejection. No prior warning is required.

3-3-1m The runner is guilty of malicious contact. The ball is dead, the runner shall be declared out and ejected. All other runners must return to last base touched at the time of the contact.

3-3-1n A player who calls time or uses any command or commits any act for the purpose of causing a balk shall be ejected.

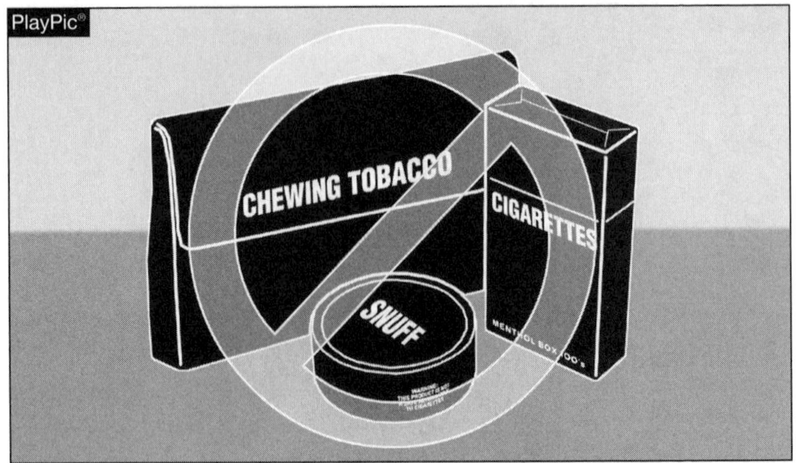

3-3-1o No tobacco or tobacco-like products are permitted within the confines of the field.

3-3-1p Any player who leaves the bench/dugout area or his position during a fight for any reason shall be ejected. Only coaches are permitted to leave their positions, and only for the purpose of breaking up the fight.

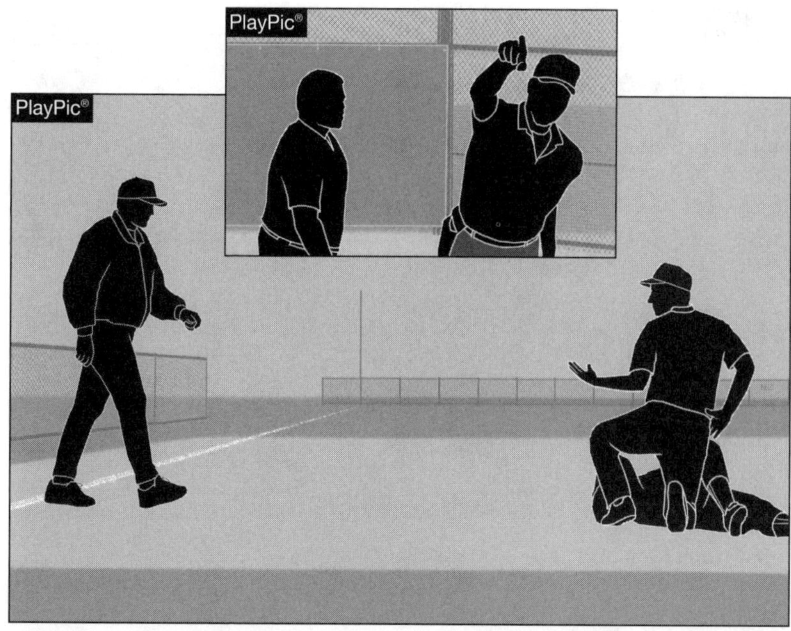

3-3-2 A coach who is ejected shall leave the vicinity of the playing area immediately and is prohibited from further contact, direct or indirect, with the team during the remainder of the game. He may return when requested to attend to an ill or injured player.

3-3-3 The umpire should direct the batter to return to his team's on-deck circle while the pitcher is warming up.

3-4-1 Each team may be granted not more than three charged defensive conferences during a seven-inning game. The umpire-in-chief shall record each conference and not permit any conferences in excess of the limit.

3-4-1 A coach or trainer attending to an injured player is not charged with a conference.

3-4-2 While on offense, each team is limited to one charged conference per inning to permit the coach or any of that team's personnel to confer with base runners, the batter, the on-deck batter or other offensive team personnel. The umpire shall deny any subsequent offensive team requests for charged conferences.

3-4-3 A defensive charged conference is concluded when the coach or non-playing representative crosses the foul line if the conference was in fair territory.

3-4-3 If a defensive charged conference was held in foul territory, the conference concludes when the coach or non-playing representative (25) initially starts to return to the dugout/bench area.

3-4-4 An offensive charged conference is concluded when the coach or team representative initially starts to return to the coach's box or dugout/bench area.

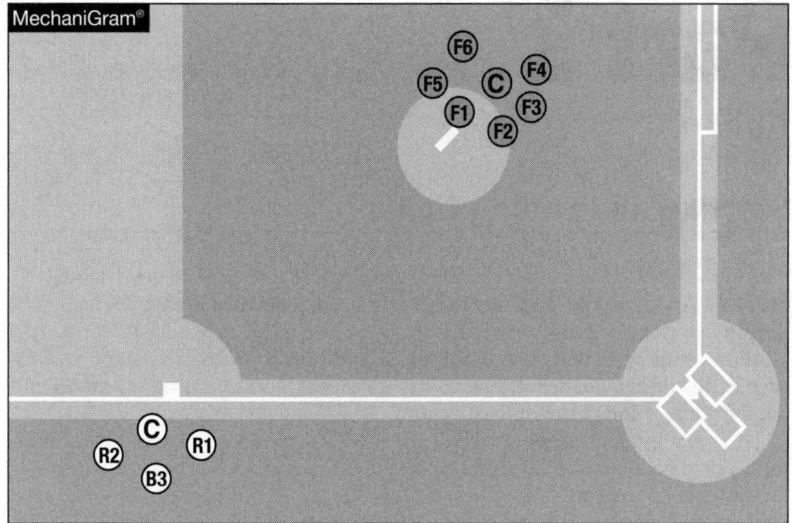

3-4-5 When either team has a charged conference, the other team may also meet. The team not charged with the conference may not cause any further delay. That meeting must conclude when the conference of the team that is charged is through with its conference.

Part 3

Rule 4

Starting and Ending Game

One of the keys to a successful baseball game is knowing how to get it started properly. And if a game doesn't finish in the correct manner, nothing else an umpire has done correctly will matter.

From suitable playing conditions to ground rules to lineup cards to who bats first … this rule covers what is necessary for those things to happen correctly and get the game going in the right direction.

A regulation high school baseball game consists of seven innings unless extra innings are necessary because of a tie score. The game can also be shortened for a number of reasons —weather, 10-run rule, not enough players, forfeit. Understanding what happens to cause those things and how the rules tell you to handle them are critical components for administering the end of a game.

4-1-1 Until the game begins, the home coach or game management shall decide whether the grounds and other conditions are suitable for starting the game.

4-1-1 Once the game has started, the umpires are sole judges as to whether conditions are fit for play and as to whether or not conditions are suitable for starting the second game of a scheduled doubleheader.

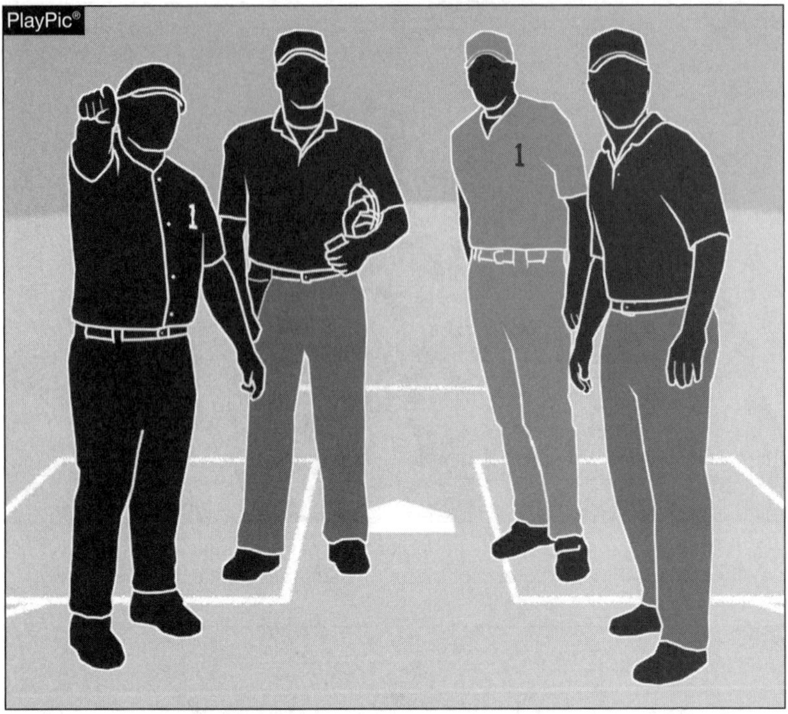

4-1-2 The home coach goes over any special ground rules necessary for his field. Proposed ground rules can not supersede a written rule. If the visiting coach disagrees with a proposed ground rule, the umpires shall formulate ground rules. All special rules shall be announced.

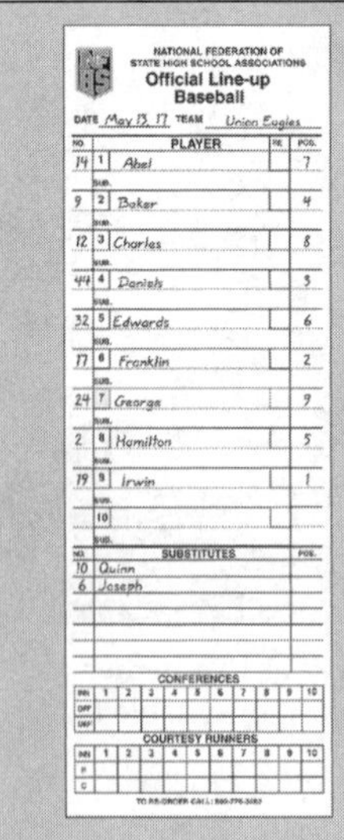
NATIONAL FEDERATION OF STATE HIGH SCHOOL ASSOCIATIONS
Official Line-up
Baseball

DATE May 13, 17 TEAM Union Eagles

NO.		PLAYER	RE	POS.
14	1	Abel		7
	SUB.			
9	2	Baker		4
	SUB.			
12	3	Charles		8
	SUB.			
44	4	Daniels		3
	SUB.			
32	5	Edwards		6
	SUB.			
17	6	Franklin		2
	SUB.			
24	7	George		9
	SUB.			
2	8	Hamilton		5
	SUB.			
19	9	Irwin		1
	SUB.			
	10			
	SUB.			

NO.	SUBSTITUTES	POS.
10	Quinn	
6	Joseph	

CONFERENCES

INN	1	2	3	4	5	6	7	8	9	10
OFF										
DEF										

COURTESY RUNNERS

INN	1	2	3	4	5	6	7	8	9	10
P										
C										

4-1-3 Before game time, the home team and then the visiting team shall deliver their respective batting orders in duplicate to the umpire-in-chief. The umpire then shall permit inspection by both head coaches and/or captains if available. Lineups become official after they have been exchanged, verified and then accepted by the umpire during the pregame conference.

4-1-3b Umpires are no longer required to inspect bats and helmets. Instead, coaches will certify at the pregame meeting that all equipment is compliant.

4-1-3b The umpire-in-chief shall receive verification from both head coaches that all participants are properly uniformed and equipped with bats that are unaltered from the original manufacturer's design and production and helmets that meet NFHS and NOCSAE standards and free of cracks or damage.

4-1-3b During the pregame conference, a coach may ask the umpires to verify the legality of an opponent's equipment. Umpires would then be required to check the equipment of that team.

4-1-3b For the first violation of the illegal bat rule by a team, the batter is called out and the head coach is restricted to the dugout/bench area for the remainder of the game.

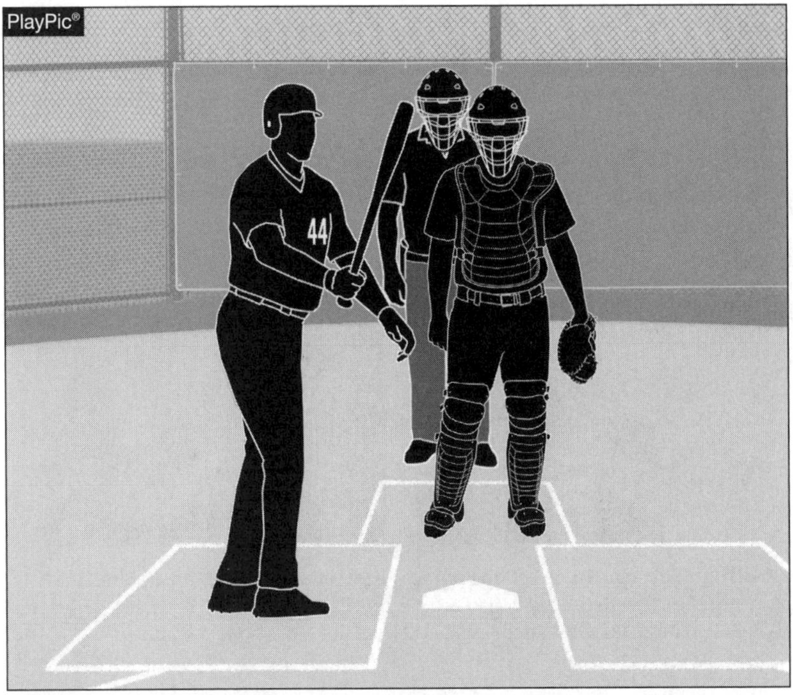

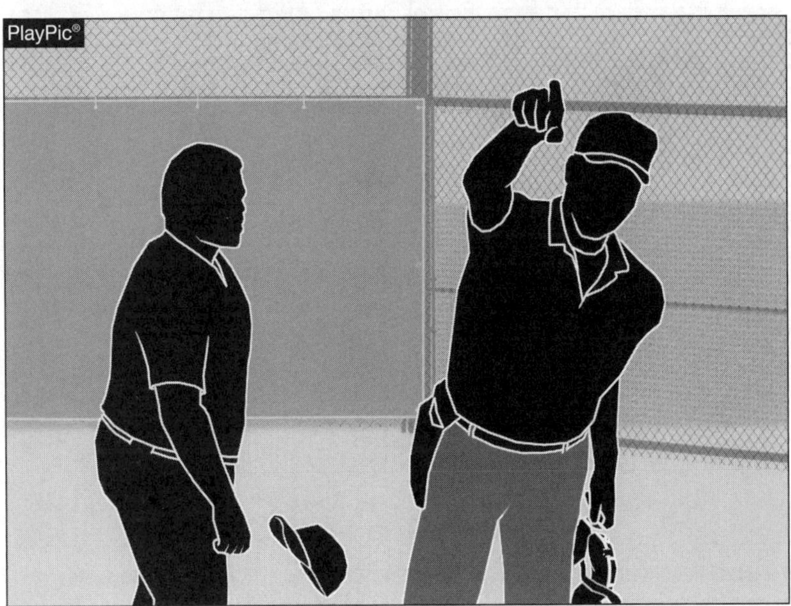

4-1-3b For a team's second illegal bat violation during a game, the batter is called out and the head coach is ejected. A batter is considered to have used a bat when he steps into the batters box.

4-1-3b For subsequent violations of the illegal bat rule in the same game, the player and designated head coach are ejected. The designated head coach is not given a warning since the team has had two prior violations penalized.

4-1-3b The penalties for using an illegal bat do not apply to using an illegal helmet. A batter must replace an illegal helmet when it is spotted, but he is not called out, nor is his coach penalized.

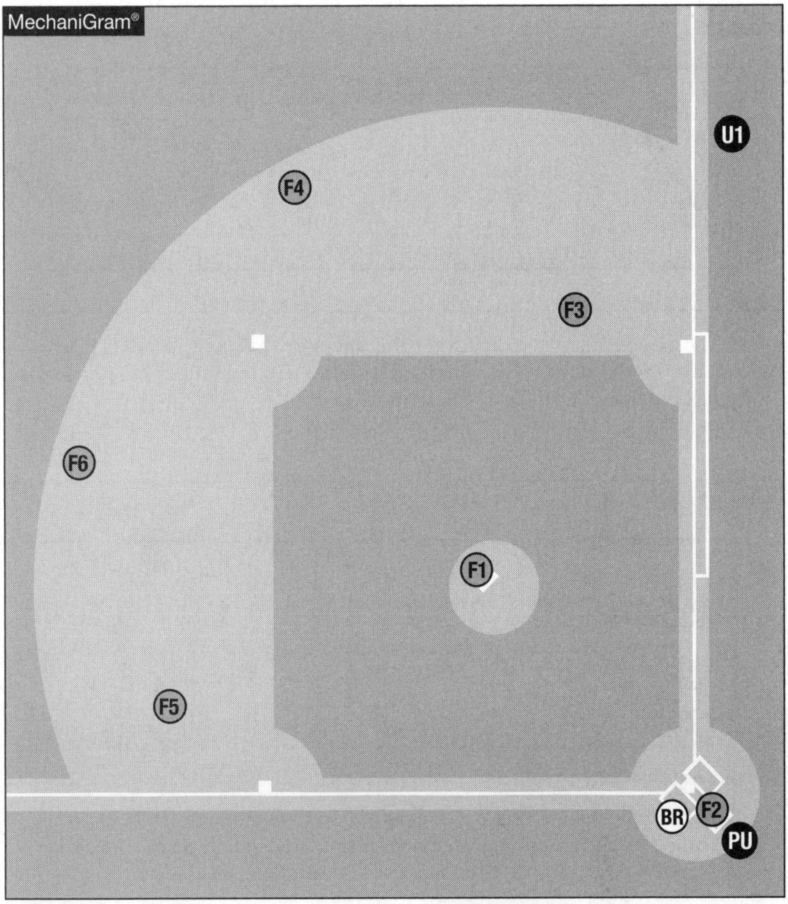

4-1-5 The game begins when the umpire calls "play" after all infielders, pitcher, catcher and batter are in position to start the game.

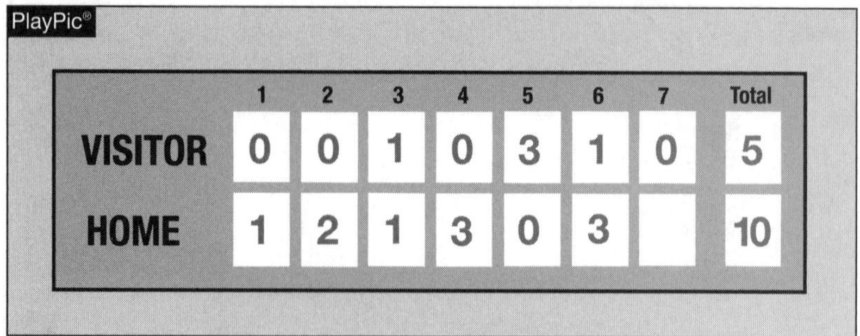

4-2-2 The game ends when the team behind in score has completed its turn at bat in the seventh inning, or any inning thereafter if extra innings are necessary. Since the home team leads 10-5, this game is over.

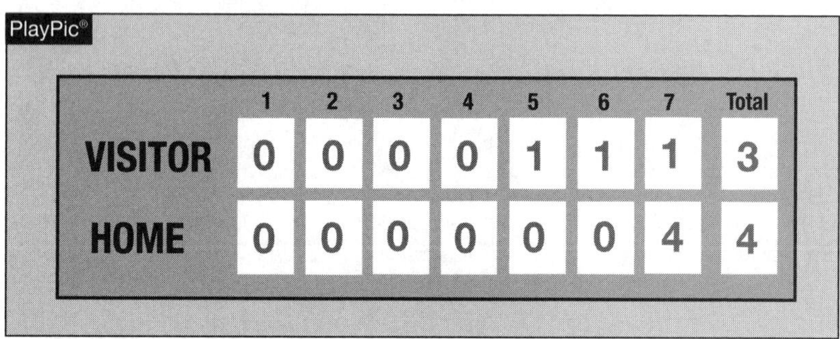

4-2-2 If the home team scores a go-ahead run in the bottom of the seventh inning, or in any extra inning, the game is terminated at that point. Once the home team scored the fourth run to take a 4-3 lead, the game is over.

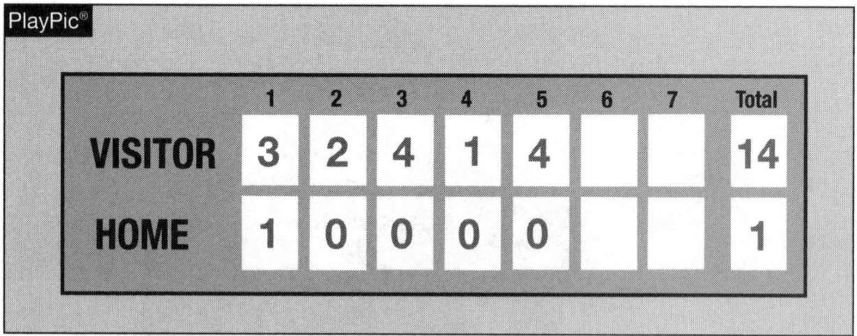

4-2-2 By state association adoption, the game shall end when the visiting team is behind 10 or more runs after 4 1/2 innings, or after the fifth inning, if either team is 10 runs behind and both teams have had an equal number of times at bat. The visiting team leads, 14-1, after five innings, so the game is over.

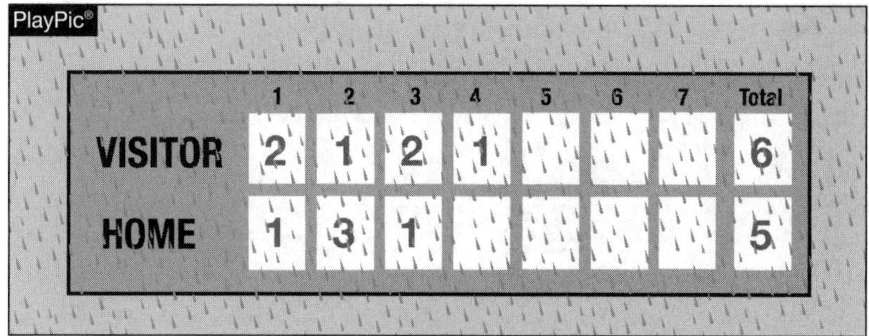

4-2-3a A game becomes regulation when five full innings have been played, or if the home team has scored an equal or greater number of runs in four or four and a fraction innings than the visiting team has scored in five innings. This game is in the fourth inning, so it is not a regulation game.

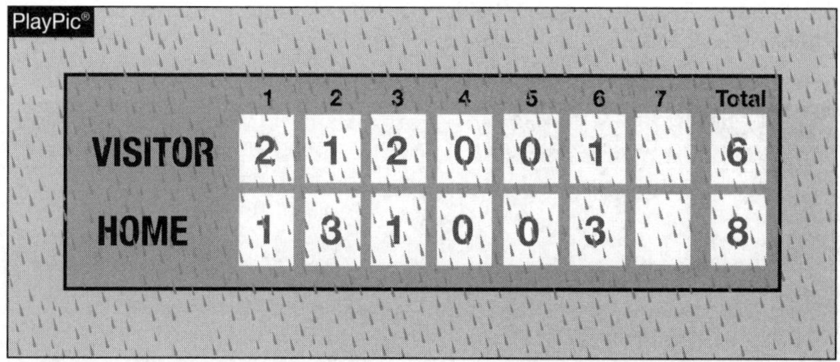

4-2-3b This game has gone more than five innings and the home team is leading, 8-6. This game would be a completed regulation game unless the state association has adopted a game ending procedure.

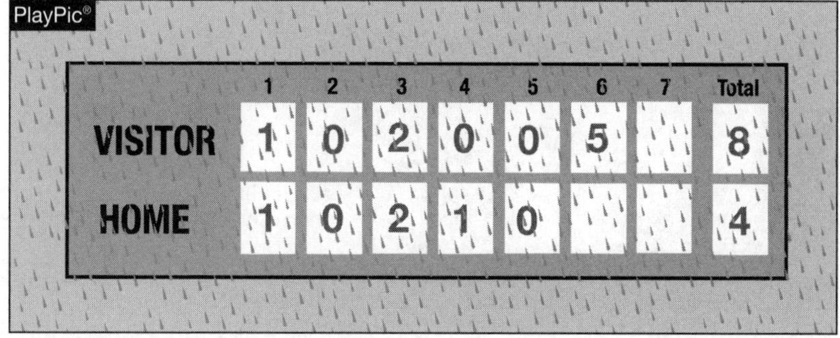

4-2-3 Since the home team hasn't batted in its half of the sixth inning, the score reverts to the last completed inning, so the home team would win, 4-3, unless the state association has adopted a game ending procedure.

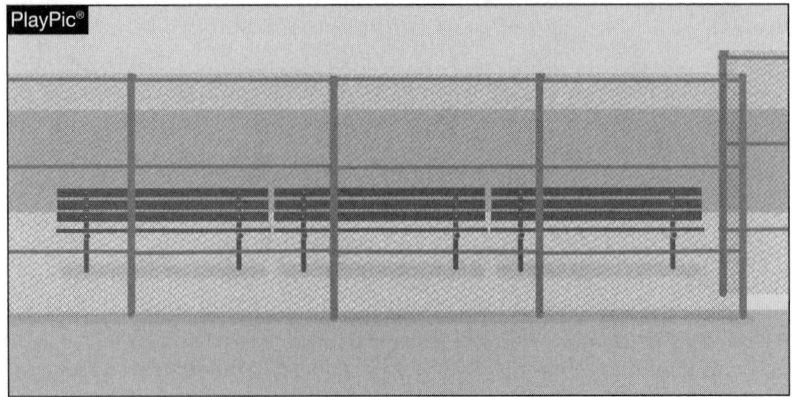

4-4-1 When a team is late in appearing, the game shall be forfeited to the offended team by the umpire. State associations are authorized to specify the time frame and/or circumstance before a forfeit will be declared for a late arrival by one of the teams.

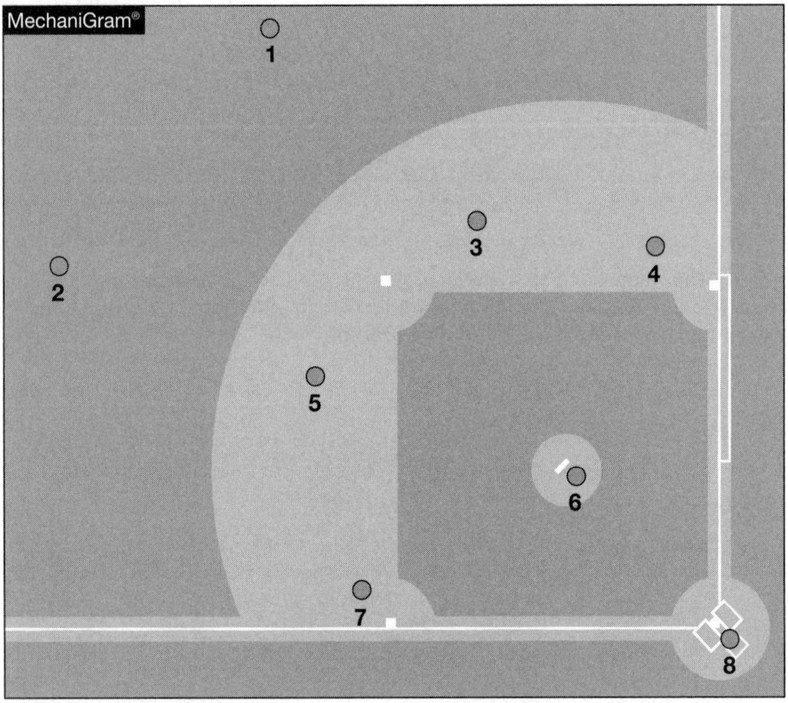

MechaniGram®

4-4-1f Teams may drop to eight players and finish a game. An out will be called each time the vacated spot in the batting order comes to bat. If an eligible player arrives, a team may return to nine players.

Part 3
Rule 5

Dead Ball – Suspension of Play

When the ball becomes dead in baseball, very few things can happen. The defense can appeal for missed bases or early tag-ups. The offense can advance to awarded bases.

There are two types of dead-ball situations in baseball — those that are dead immediately and those that become dead at the end of playing action. It is important to be able to distinguish which situation has occurred, so that any penalty may be properly applied.

This section of the rule book explains situations in which balls are immediately dead, and which ones are delayed. It also covers what can and cannot happen while the ball is dead and the proper procedure for resuming play once it has been suspended.

5-1-1a The ball becomes dead immediately when the batter (or his clothing) is hit by a pitch.

5-1-1c The ball becomes dead immediately when the batter enters the batter's box with an illegal bat. This bat is illegal because the weight/length ratio is higher than the minus-3 allowed by rule.

5-1-1d When the ball goes directly from the bat to the catcher's protector, mask or person without first touching the catcher's glove or hand, the ball is ruled foul and becomes dead immediately.

5-1-1e The runner's interference causes the ball to become dead immediately.

5-1-1f When a batted ball touches an umpire before touching any fielder and before passing any fielder other than the pitcher, the ball becomes dead immediately.

5-1-1f A fielder is not allowed to toss a glove with a lodged ball in an attempt to make a play.

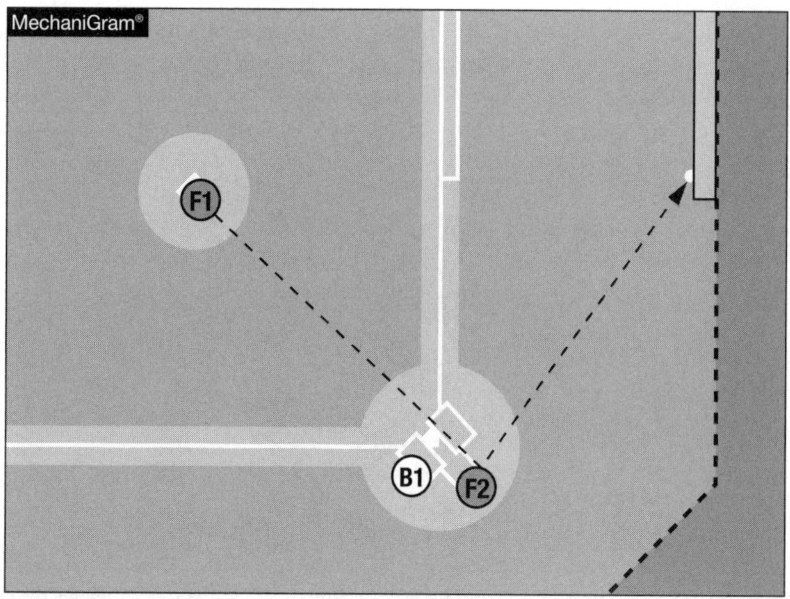

5-1-1g When a pitch or any thrown ball goes into a stand or other dead-ball area or players' bench, the ball becomes dead immediately, even if it rebounds back into live-ball territory.

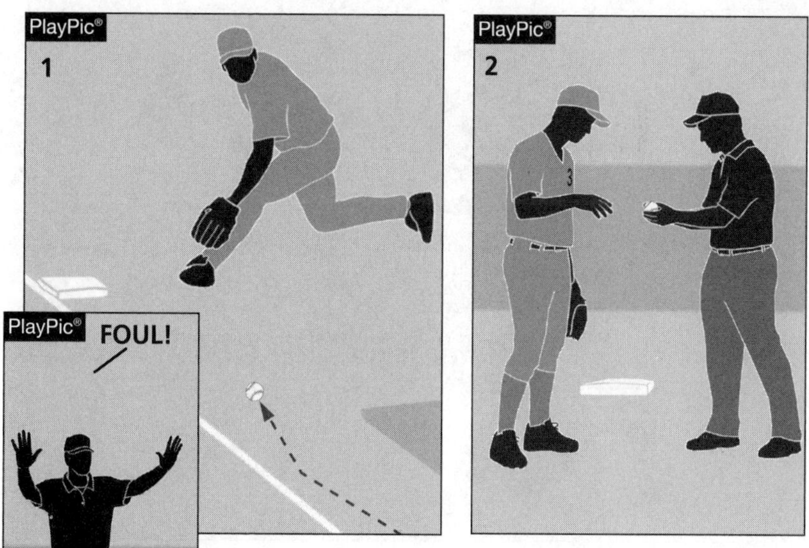

5-1-1h When the umpire inadvertently announces foul on a grounded ball (PlayPic 1) or handles a live ball (PlayPic 2), the ball becomes dead immediately.

5-1-1i After catching a fair or foul ball (fly or line drive), if the fielder leaves the field of play by stepping with both feet into dead-ball territory, the ball becomes dead.

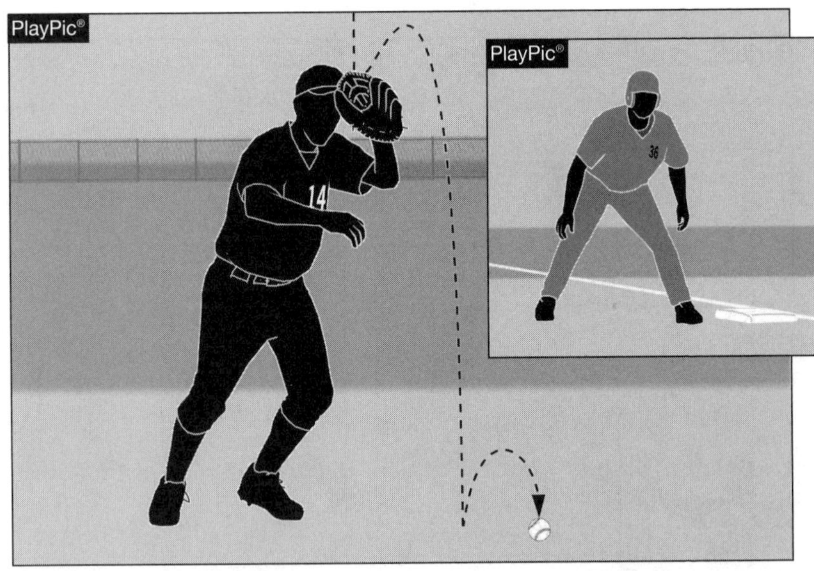

5-1-1j When an infielder intentionally drops a fair fly with at least first base occupied and with less than two outs, the ball is dead immediately. **Exception:** When the infield fly rule is in effect.

5-1-1k The ball becomes dead immediately when a balk or an illegal pitch is committed.

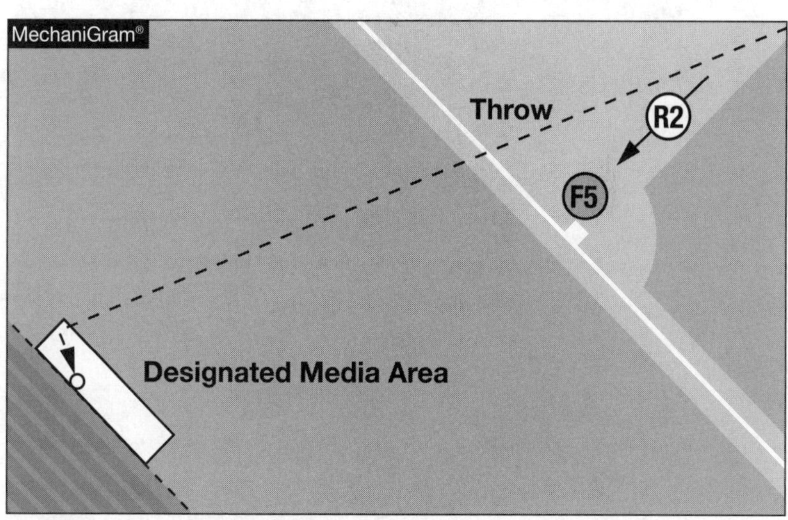

5-1-1l When the ball touches a designated media area or anyone or anything that is entirely or partially in the designated media area, it becomes dead immediately. If the ball passes through the media area, but doesn't touch it, it remains live.

5-1-2b When a fielder or catcher obstructs the ball through use of detached player equipment, it is a delayed-dead ball.

5-1-2c It is a delayed-dead ball when the umpire interferes with the catcher who is attempting to throw.

5-1-2d The act of calling time in an attempt to cause the opposing pitcher to balk is a delayed-dead ball.

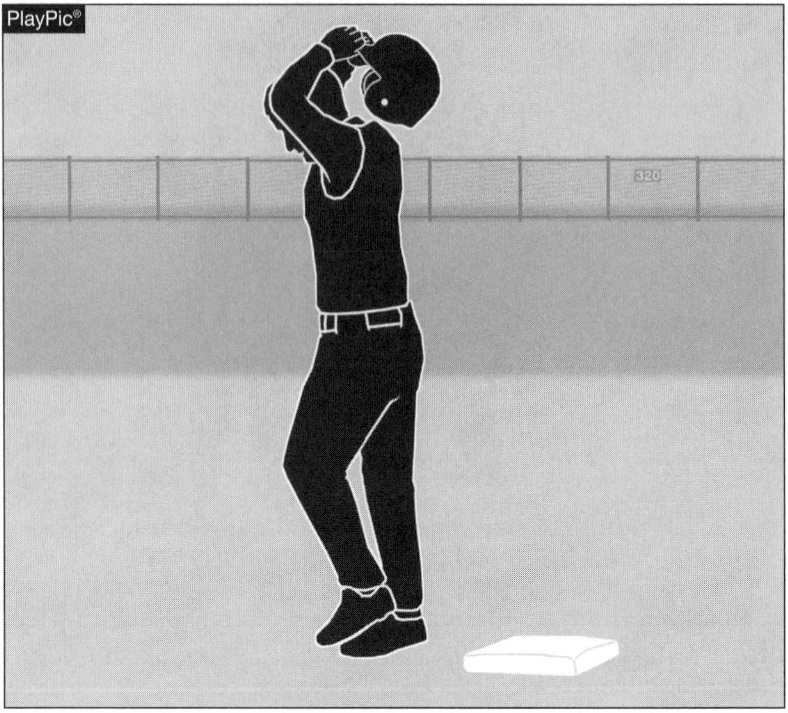

5-1-2e When anyone who is required to wear a batting helmet deliberately removes it while the ball is live, it is a delayed-dead ball.

5-1-2f The first baseman is wearing a catcher's mitt. It is a delayed-dead ball when a ball touches an illegal glove or mitt.

5-1-4 After a dead ball, the ball becomes live when it is held by the pitcher in a legal pitching position, provided the pitcher has engaged the pitcher's plate, the batter and the catcher are in their respective boxes, and the umpire puts the ball in play and gives the appropriate hand signal.

5-2-1b When the umpire considers the weather or ground conditions unfit for play, time shall be called and the game suspended. **Note:** After 30 minutes, the umpire may declare the game ended.

5-2-1c When a spectator is ordered from the grounds, time shall be called and the game suspended.

5-2-1d When an injury occurs during a live ball, time shall not be called until no further advance or putout is possible. If there is a medical emergency or if, in the umpire's judgment, further play could jeopardize the injured player's safety, play should be stopped immediately.

5-2-2a The umpire called time (PlayPic 1) prior to the fielder applying this tag (PlayPic 2). When the ball becomes dead, no action by the defense can cause a player to be put out, unless they are making a proper dead-ball appeal.

5-2-2b When the ball becomes dead, a runner may return to a base he left too soon on a caught fly ball or that was not touched during a live ball. **Exception:** A runner who is on or beyond a succeeding base when the ball became dead, or advances and touches a succeeding base after the ball became dead, may not return and shall be called out upon proper and successful appeal (8-2-5).

Part 3
Rule 6

Pitching

The pitch can be thrown from either of two basic positions — the windup or the set position. This rule explains the pitcher's positioning and what he can do from each of those positions.

Just as important, however, are the things a pitcher cannot do, either from one of the two positions, or at any time, regardless of whether he is using the set or windup. There are 20 infractions listed that a pitcher can commit, with penalties ranging from a warning to ejection.

This rule also explains that while a pitcher is not pitching, he is treated like any other infielder, except that when a ball passes the pitcher, it can still become dead when it strikes an umpire or a baserunner.

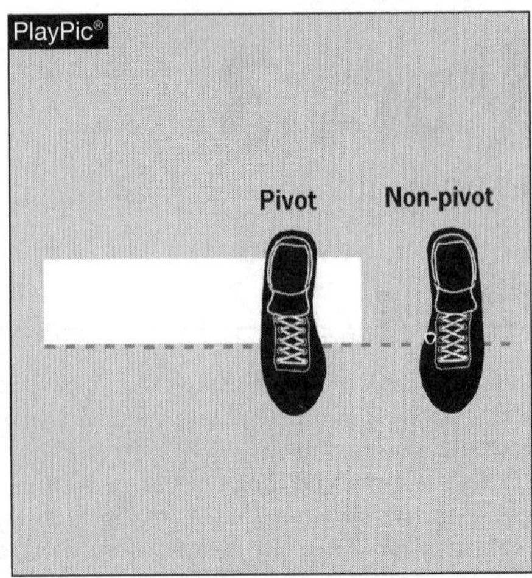

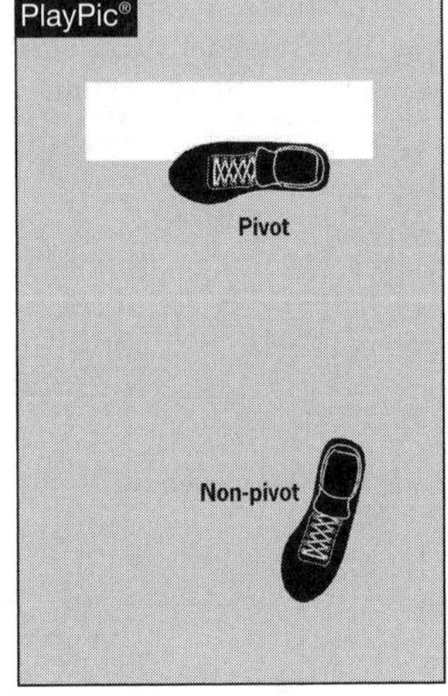

6-1-1 The pitcher shall pitch while facing the batter from either a windup position (PlayPic 1) or a set position (PlayPic 2). The position of his feet determine whether he will pitch from the windup or the set position.

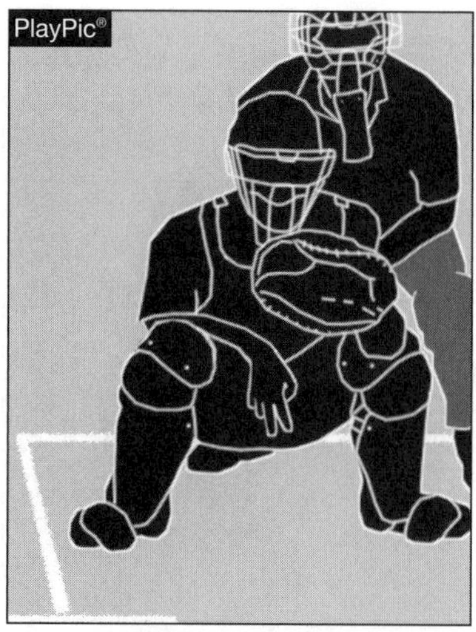

6-1-1 The pitcher shown here is committing a violation by taking his signs from in front of the rubber. Pitchers are required to take their signs from the catcher with his pivot foot in contact with the pitcher's plate.

6-1-1 Turning the shoulders to check runners while in contact with the pitcher's plate in the set position is legal.

6-1-1 Turning the shoulders after bringing the hands together during or after the stretch is a balk.

6-1-1 If a pitcher is ambidextrous, the umpire shall require the pitcher to face a batter as either a left-handed pitcher or right-handed pitcher, but not both. This pitcher would not be allowed to switch hands during the middle of a batter's plate appearance.

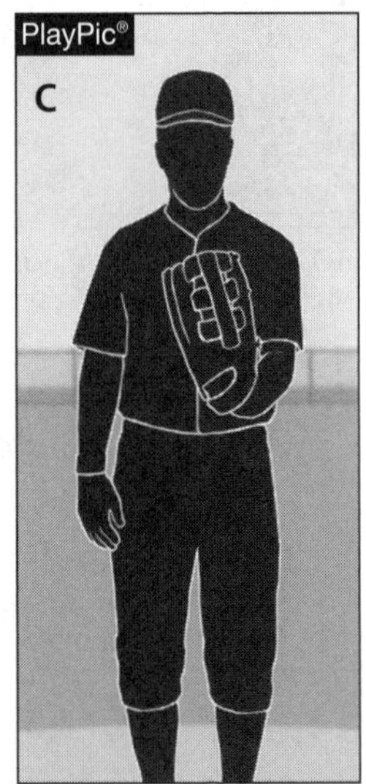

6-1-2 A pitcher assumes the windup position when his hands are: (a) together in front of the body; (b) both hands are at his side; (c) either hand is in front of the body and the other hand is at his side.

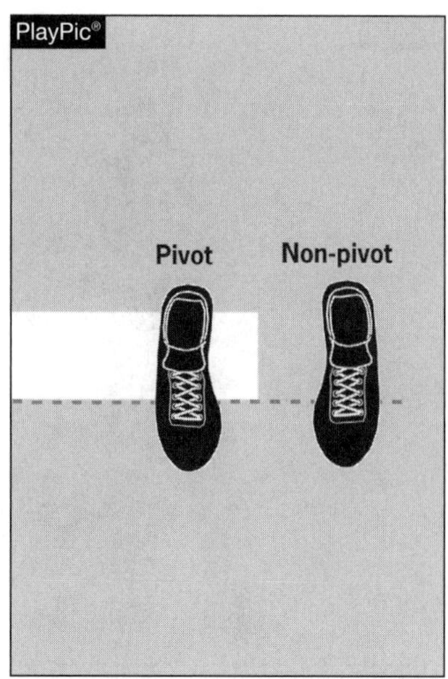

6-1-2 The windup is one of two legal pitching positions. For the windup, the pitcher's non-pivot foot shall be in any position on or behind a line extending through the front edge of the pitcher's plate.

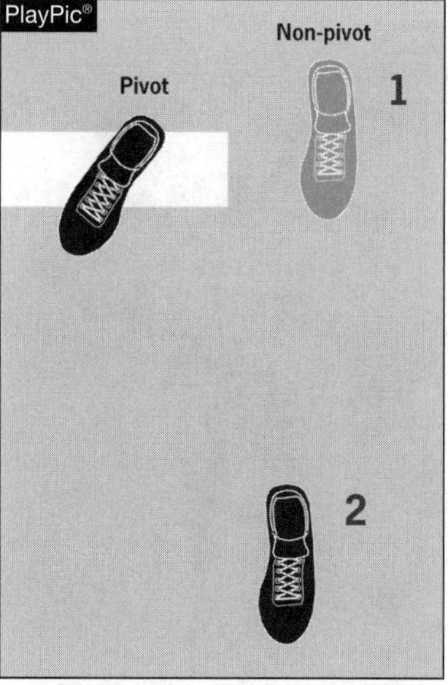

6-1-2 During delivery from the windup position, a pitcher may lift his non-pivot foot in a step forward, with no other steps, and throw a pitch. Once he has moved his non-pivot foot, he is committed to pitch.

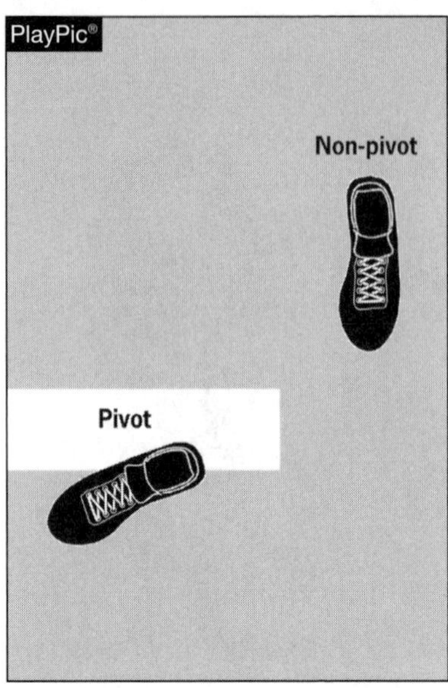

6-1-2 During delivery from the windup position, the pitcher may begin the pitching motion with a step backward. Once he has moved his non-pivot foot, he is committed to pitch.

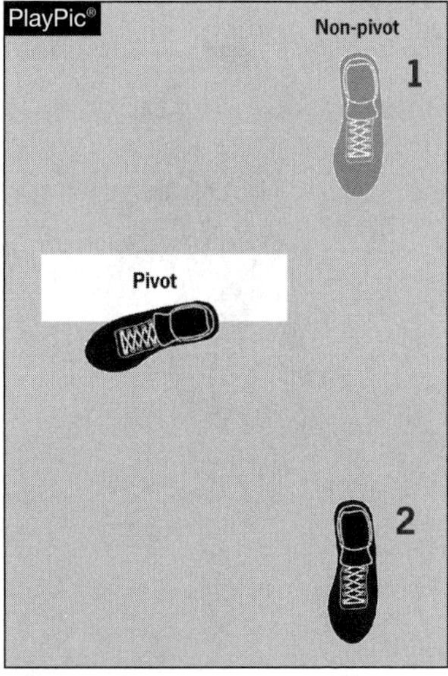

6-1-2 The most common move for a pitcher from the windup position is a step backward and then a step forward. This is a legal move; however, he is committed to pitch when he moves his non-pivot foot.

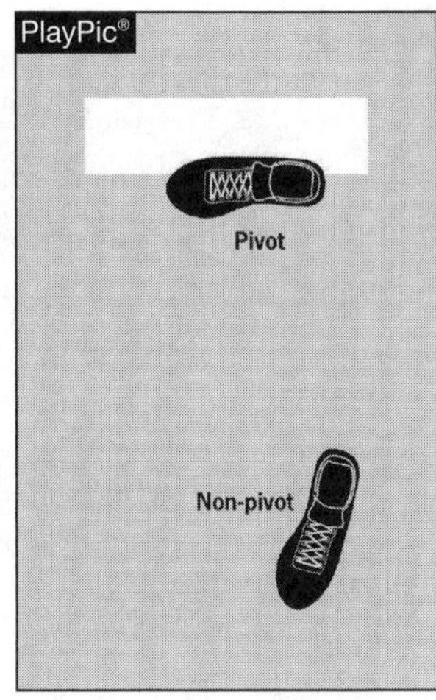

6-1-3 The set is one of two legal pitching positions. For the set position, a pitcher shall stand with his entire non-pivot foot in front of a line extending through the front edge of the pitcher's plate and with his entire pivot foot in contact with or directly in front of and parallel to the pitcher's plate.

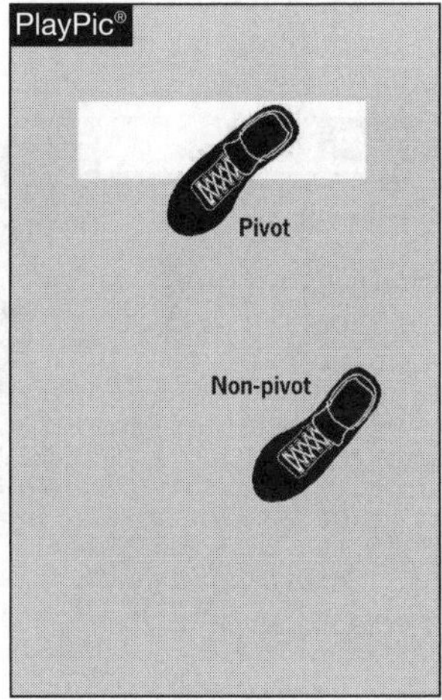

6-1-3 A number of pitchers are starting in this position and coming set. This is not a legal position because it does not meet the requirements of either the windup or set position.

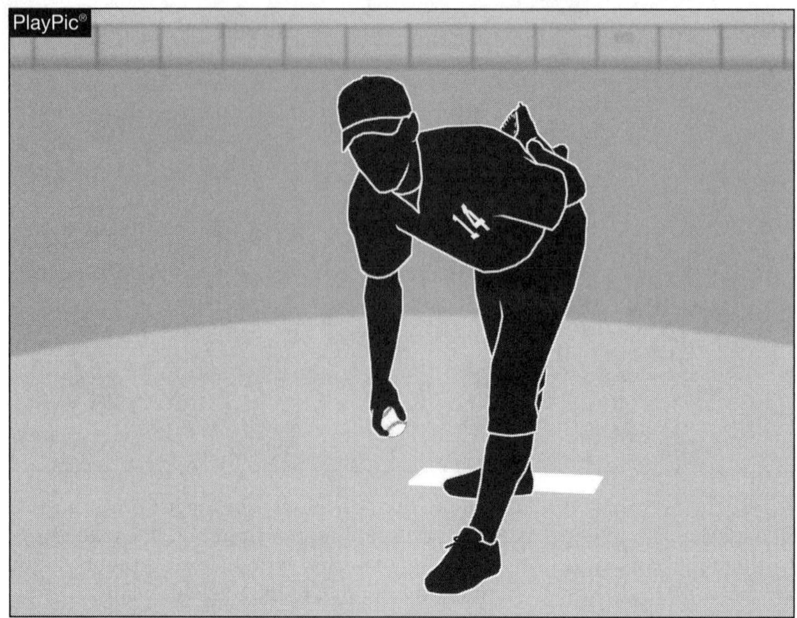

6-1-3 As long as his arm is not swinging, the pitcher is allowed to have his arm hanging by his side. Any swinging motion of the arm constitutes the beginning of the pitching motion.

6-1-5 A ball thrown by a pitcher when his pivot foot is not on the rubber is treated as if it was thrown by an infielder.

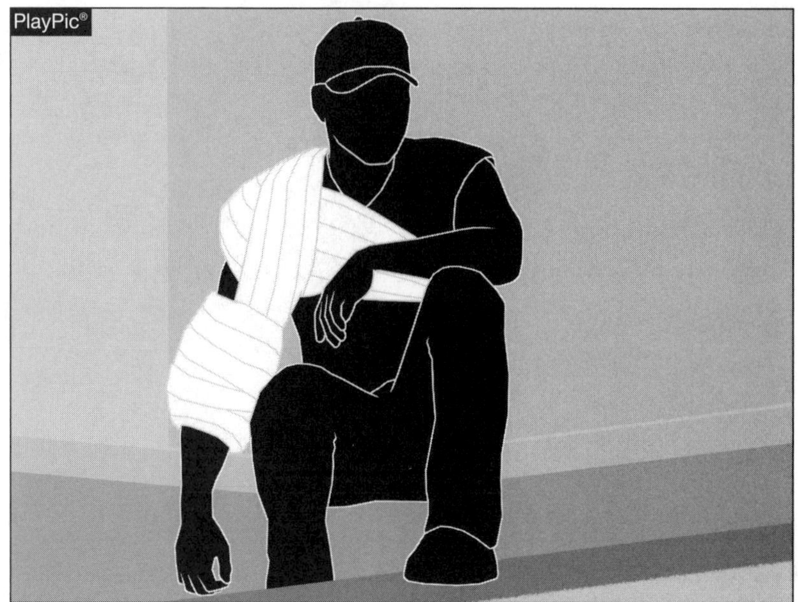

6-1-6 Each state association shall have a pitching restriction policy based on the number of pitches thrown to afford pitchers a required rest period between pitching appearances.

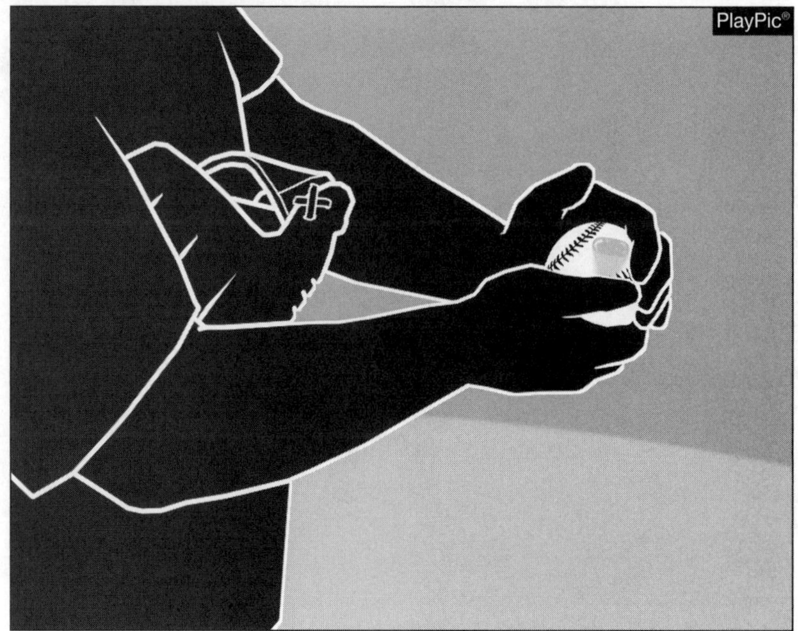

6-2-1a A pitcher may not apply a foreign substance to the ball.

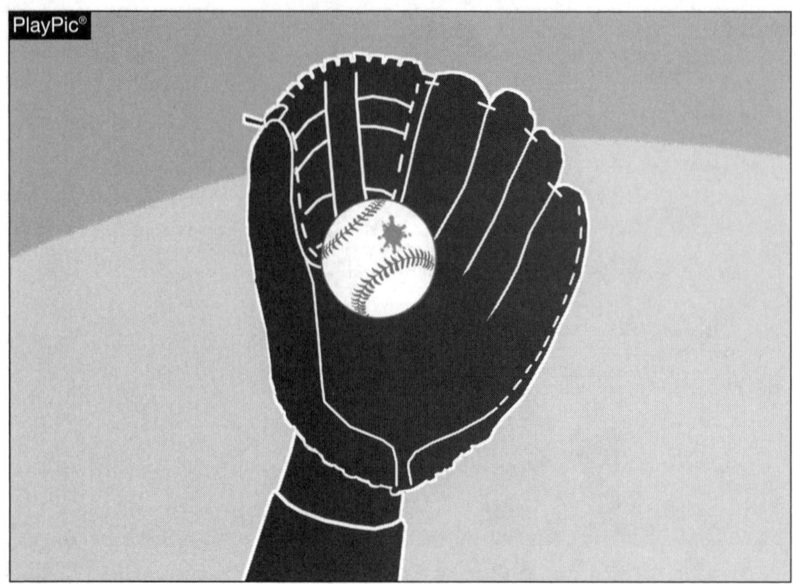

6-2-1b Spitting on the ball or glove is illegal.

6-2-1c Rubbing the ball on the glove, clothing or person is illegal if the act defaces the ball.

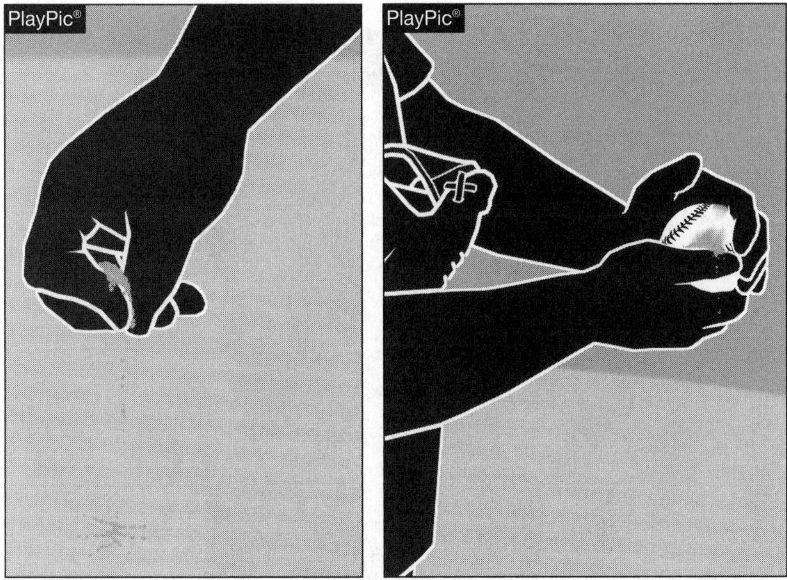

6-2-1d The pitcher may not discolor the ball with dirt. He may rub the ball with his bare hands to remove any extraneous coating.

6-2-1e The pitcher shall not bring the pitching hand in contact with the mouth without distinctly wiping off the pitching hand before it touches the ball. The pitcher shown here has not done anything illegal, because he wiped his pitching hand off before it touched the ball.

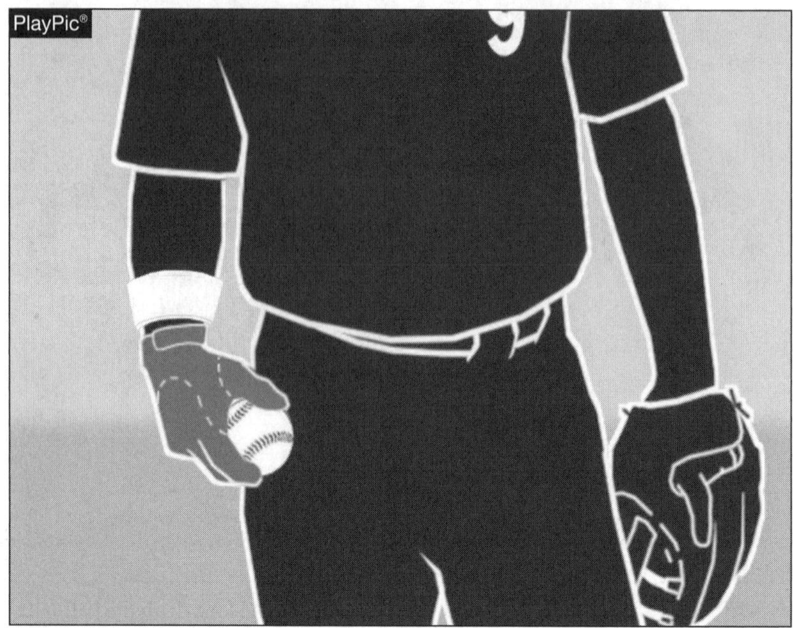

6-2-1f Pitchers may not wear anything on their hands, wrists or arms that may be distracting to the batter.

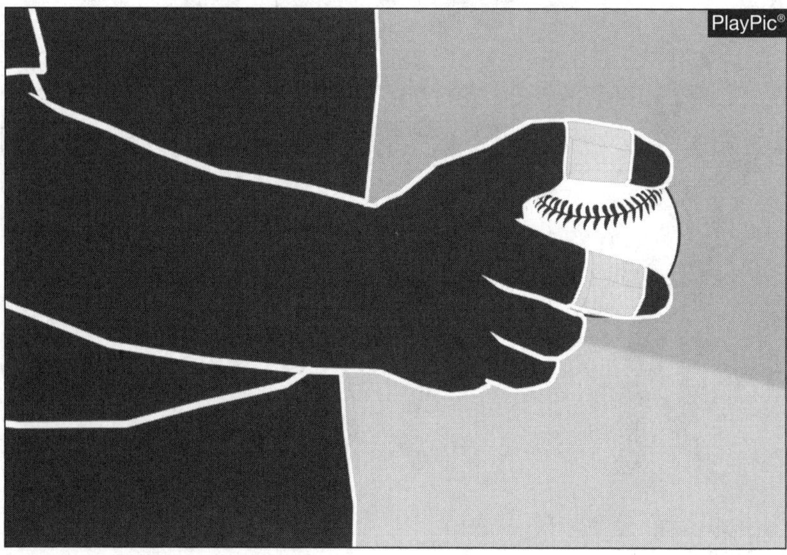

6-2-1g The pitcher shall not wear tape, bandages or other foreign material (other than rosin) on the fingers or palm of his pitching hand that could come in contact with the ball.

6-2-1h The pitcher may not wear a glove or mitt that includes the colors white or gray.

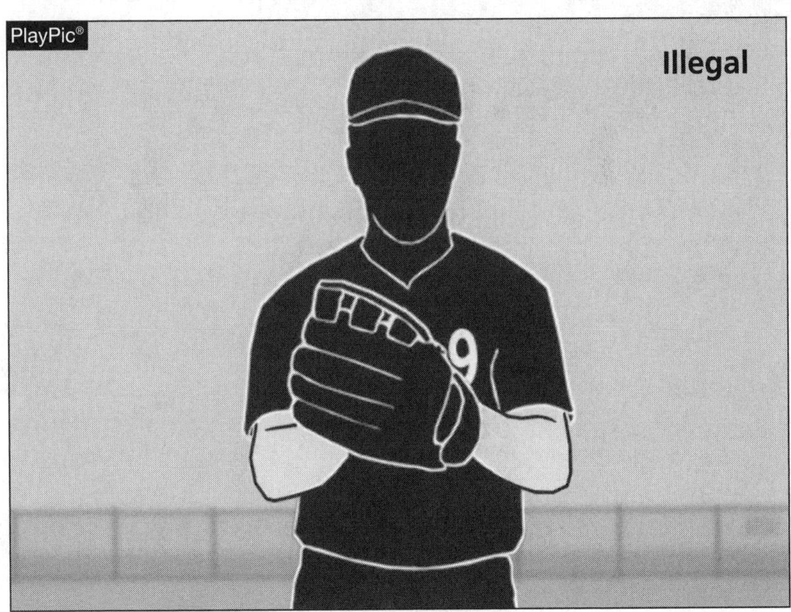

6-2-1i The pitcher shall not wear an exposed undershirt with long sleeves that are white or gray.

6-2-1 Penalty A balk (with runners on) or an illegal pitch (with no runners) is called anytime that a pitcher goes to his mouth while on the pitching plate.

6-2-2a The pitcher shall not throw to any player other than the catcher when the batter is in the batter's box, unless it is an attempt to retire a runner. This throw to an unoccupied base is illegal, since there is no possible play at the base.

6-2-2b Once a defensive team has been charged with three conferences, any further meetings are a delay of the game and the pitcher must be replaced.

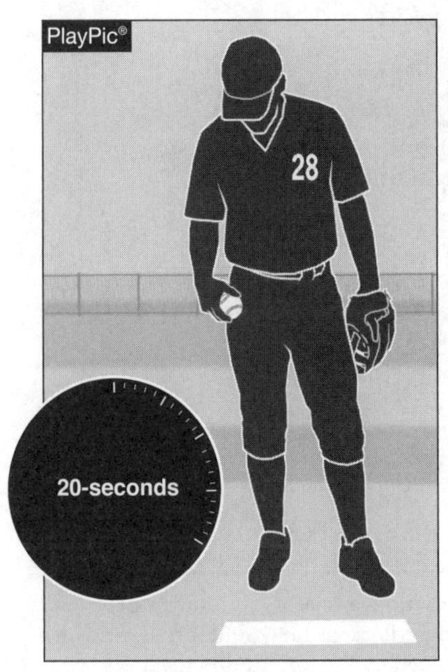

6-2-2c A pitcher must pitch or make or attempt a play, including a legal feint, within 20 seconds after he has received the ball.

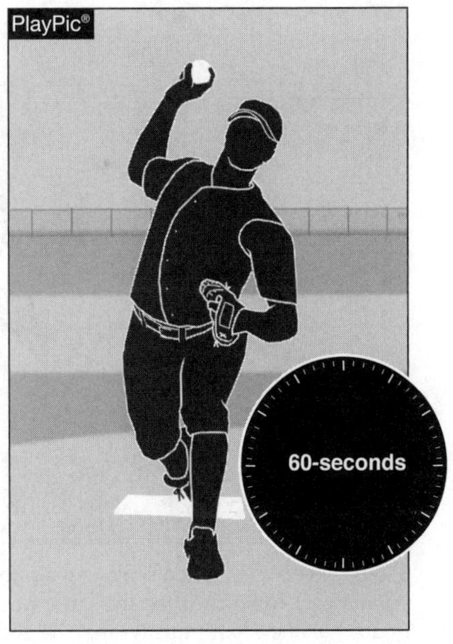

6-2-2c Except. A pitcher must complete his warm-up pitches within one minute timed from the first throw or from the third out of the previous half-inning.

6-2-2c Exception When replacing a pitcher who was ejected, the substitute pitcher should be afforded the same warmup criteria as he would if replacing an injured pitcher. Extra throws may be authorized by the umpire-in-chief.

6-2-3 The penalty for pitching intentionally close to a batter has not changed. The pitcher shall be ejected if the pitch is judged to be intentional. In case of doubt, the umpire may warn the pitcher.

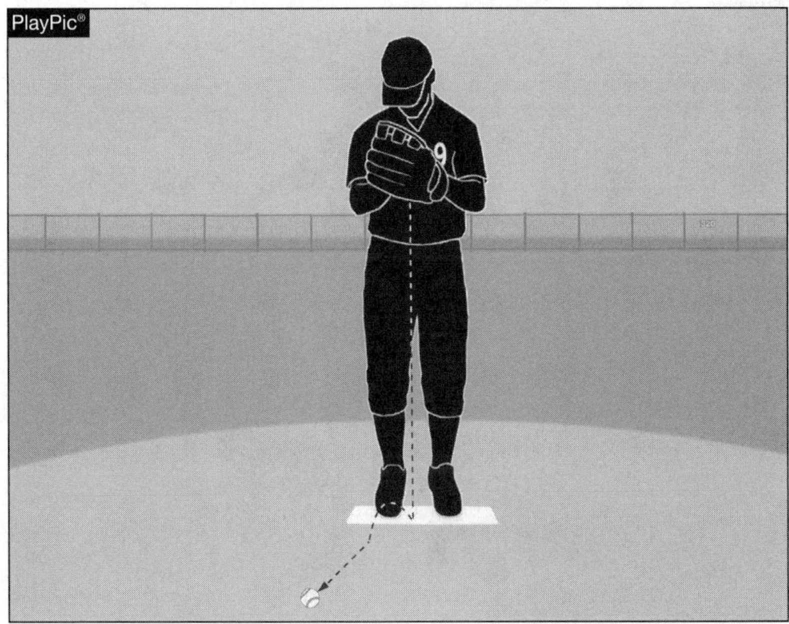

6-2-4a When the pitcher drops the ball (even accidentally) and the ball does not cross a foul line, he has committed a balk if there are runner(s) on base.

6-2-4b The pitcher has committed a balk because he did not step directly toward first base when he attempted to pick off the runner.

6-2-4d Once the pitcher has started any movement of any part of the body such as he habitually uses in his delivery, (PlayPic 1) he must complete the pitch. Failure to do so with runner(s) on base is a balk. However, if the pitcher stops or hesitates because the batter requests time or steps out of the batter's box (PlayPic 2), it is not a balk.

6-2-4e Once a pitcher in the set position has come to a stretch, he may not take his hand out of the glove without the ball, unless he steps off the pitcher's plate, pitches to the batter, throws to a base or steps toward and feints a throw to second or third base. The pitcher shown here is in the set position (PlayPic 1) and brought the ball and his glove hand together in front of his body legally (PlayPic 2). He then removed his hand from the glove without the ball (PlayPic 3). With a runner on base, this would be a balk.

6-2-4f Once the pitcher's entire non-pivot foot passes behind the perpendicular plane of the back edge of the pitcher's plate, the pitcher must either pitch or throw/feint to second base in an attempt to put out a runner. Since this pitcher is throwing or feinting toward third base, this is a balk.

6-2-5 A pitcher may not position himself within approximately five feet of the pitcher's plate without the ball with a runner(s) on base.

6-2-5 If the pitcher makes any movement normally associated with his pitch, such as taking a sign, while not in contact with the rubber, he has committed a balk.

Part 3
Rule 7

Batting

Players on offense are categorized first as a batter, then as a runner. This rule covers the first of those two categories.

The batting order is established at the start of a game, and there are penalties for not following the correct order throughout the game.

This rule also provides the six different ways a batter can be charged with a strike on a given pitch. Should a pitch not meet any of the six criteria for being a strike and not be put into play or pitching violation, it is a ball.

There are also restrictions on the batter's actions, and appropriate penalties.

NATIONAL FEDERATION OF
STATE HIGH SCHOOL ASSOCIATIONS

Official Line-up
Baseball

DATE May. 7 17 TEAM Union Eagles

NO.		PLAYER	RE	POS.
14	1	Abel		7
	SUB.			
9	2	Baker		4
	SUB.			
12	3	Charles		8
	SUB.			
44	4	Daniels		3
	SUB.			
32	5	Edwards		6
	SUB.			
17	6	Franklin		2
	SUB.			
24	7	George		9
	SUB.			
2	8	Hamilton		5
	SUB.			
19	9	Irwin		1
	SUB.			
	10			
	SUB.			

NO.	SUBSTITUTES	POS.
6	Jackson	
11	Knutson	
28	Larson	
35	Matthewson	
1	Nelson	

CONFERENCES

INN	1	2	3	4	5	6	7	8	9	10
OFF										
DEF										

COURTESY RUNNERS

INN	1	2	3	4	5	6	7	8	9	10
P										
C										

TO RE-ORDER CALL: 800-776-3462

7-1-1 The batting order established at the beginning of the game shall be followed during the entire game except that an entering substitute shall take the replaced player's place in the batting order.

A batter is in proper order if he follows the player whose name precedes his in the lineup. An improper batter is considered to be at bat as soon as he is in the batter's box and the ball is live.

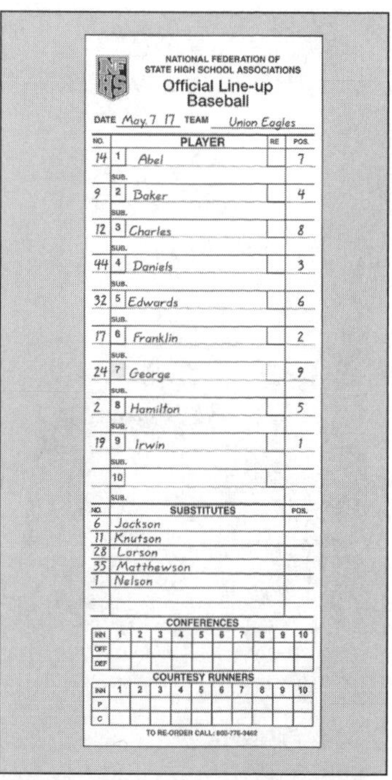

NATIONAL FEDERATION OF STATE HIGH SCHOOL ASSOCIATIONS

Official Line-up
Baseball

DATE May 7 17 TEAM Union Eagles

NO.		PLAYER	RE	POS.
14	1	Abel		7
	SUB.			
9	2	Baker		4
	SUB.			
12	3	Charles		8
	SUB.			
44	4	Daniels		3
	SUB.			
32	5	Edwards		6
	SUB.			
17	6	Franklin		2
	SUB.			
24	7	George		9
	SUB.			
2	8	Hamilton		5
	SUB.			
19	9	Irwin		1
	SUB.			
	10			
	SUB.			

NO.	SUBSTITUTES	POS.
6	Jackson	
11	Knutson	
28	Larson	
35	Matthewson	
1	Nelson	

CONFERENCES

INN	1	2	3	4	5	6	7	8	9	10
OFF										
DEF										

COURTESY RUNNERS

INN	1	2	3	4	5	6	7	8	9	10
P										
C										

TO RE-ORDER CALL: 800-776-3462

7-1-1 Penalty 2 Edwards has reached first base, and the defensive coach properly appeals that Edwards batted out of turn. The plate umpire rules that Daniels, the proper batter, is out.

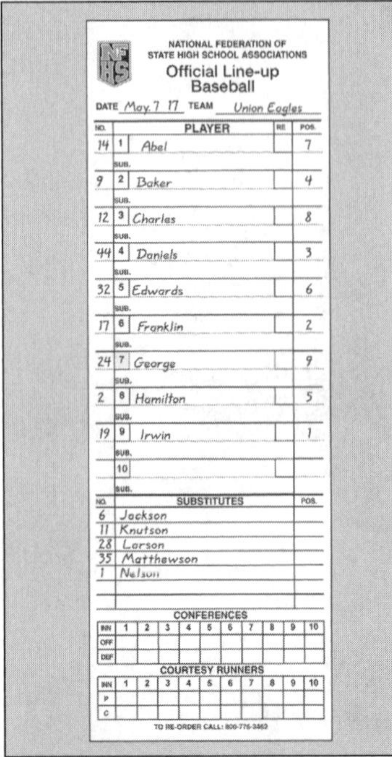

NATIONAL FEDERATION OF STATE HIGH SCHOOL ASSOCIATIONS

Official Line-up Baseball

DATE May. 7 17 TEAM Union Eagles

NO.		PLAYER	RE	POS.
14	1	Abel		7
	SUB.			
9	2	Baker		4
	SUB.			
12	3	Charles		8
	SUB.			
44	4	Daniels		3
	SUB.			
32	5	Edwards		6
	SUB.			
17	6	Franklin		2
	SUB.			
24	7	George		9
	SUB.			
2	8	Hamilton		5
	SUB.			
19	9	Irwin		1
	SUB.			
	10			
	SUB.			

NO.	SUBSTITUTES	POS.
6	Jackson	
11	Knutson	
28	Larson	
35	Matthewson	
1	Nelson	

CONFERENCES

INN	1	2	3	4	5	6	7	8	9	10
OFF										
DEF										

COURTESY RUNNERS

INN	1	2	3	4	5	6	7	8	9	10
P										
C										

TO RE-ORDER CALL: 800-776-3462

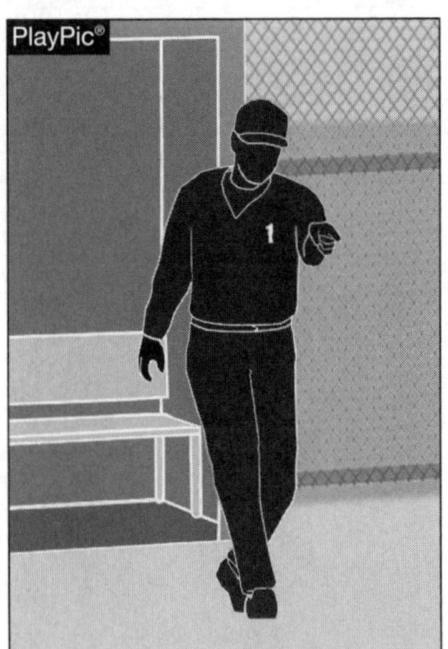

7-1-1 Penalty 3 Once a pitch has been delivered to the succeeding batter, no appeal for batting out of order shall be granted. Even though the coach wants to appeal that Daniels is on base and was an improper batter, there has already been one pitch to Edwards. The appeal, even if it is correct, shall not be granted.

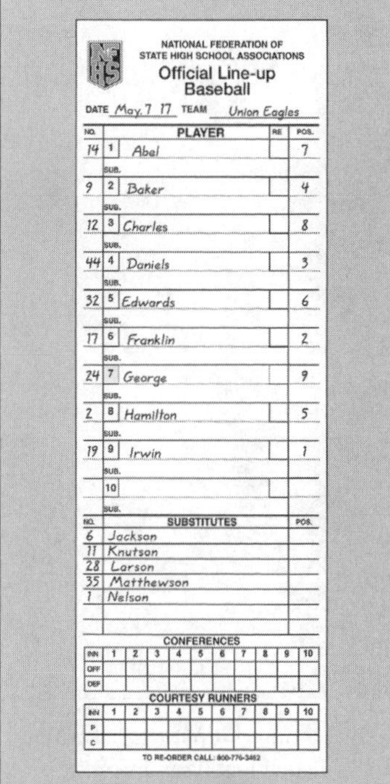

NATIONAL FEDERATION OF STATE HIGH SCHOOL ASSOCIATIONS

Official Line-up Baseball

DATE May. 7 17 TEAM Union Eagles

NO.		PLAYER	RE	POS.
14	1	Abel		7
	SUB.			
9	2	Baker		4
	SUB.			
12	3	Charles		8
	SUB.			
44	4	Daniels		3
	SUB.			
32	5	Edwards		6
	SUB.			
17	6	Franklin		2
	SUB.			
24	7	George		9
	SUB.			
2	8	Hamilton		5
	SUB.			
19	9	Irwin		1
	SUB.			
	10			
	SUB.			

NO.	SUBSTITUTES	POS.
6	Jackson	
11	Knutson	
28	Larson	
35	Matthewson	
1	Nelson	

CONFERENCES

INN	1	2	3	4	5	6	7	8	9	10
OFF										
DEF										

COURTESY RUNNERS

INN	1	2	3	4	5	6	7	8	9	10
P										
C										

TO RE-ORDER CALL: 800-776-3462

7-1-1 Penalty 4 Edwards batted out of order. Following a proper appeal prior to the next pitch, Daniels, who was the proper batter, is called out and Edwards is removed from first base. Edwards is now the proper batter.

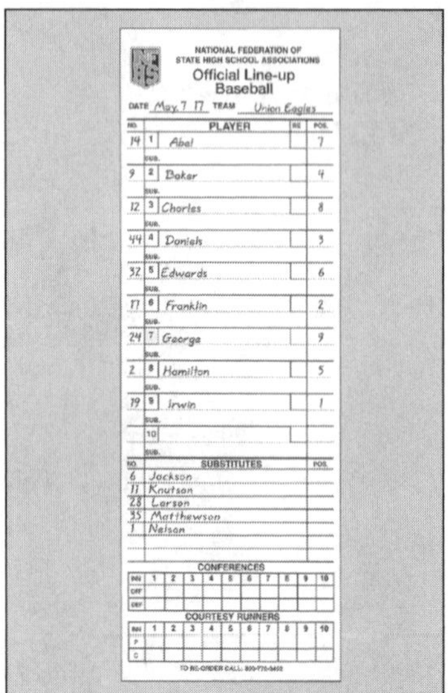

NATIONAL FEDERATION OF STATE HIGH SCHOOL ASSOCIATIONS

Official Line-up
Baseball

DATE May. 7 17 TEAM Union Eagles

NO.		PLAYER	RE	POS.
14	1	Abel		7
	SUB.			
9	2	Baker		4
	SUB.			
12	3	Charles		8
	SUB.			
44	4	Daniels		3
	SUB.			
32	5	Edwards		6
	SUB.			
17	6	Franklin		2
	SUB.			
24	7	George		9
	SUB.			
2	8	Hamilton		5
	SUB.			
19	9	Irwin		1
	SUB.			
	10			
	SUB.			

NO.	SUBSTITUTES	POS.
6	Jackson	
11	Knutson	
28	Larson	
35	Matthewson	
1	Nelson	

CONFERENCES

INN	1	2	3	4	5	6	7	8	9	10
OFF										
DEF										

COURTESY RUNNERS

INN	1	2	3	4	5	6	7	8	9	10
P										
C										

TO RE-ORDER CALL:

7-1-1 Penalty 5 When no legal appeal is made for batting out of order, the next batter shall be the batter whose name follows that of such legalized improper batter. Edwards batted out of order, but no appeal was made. The next legal batter is Franklin.

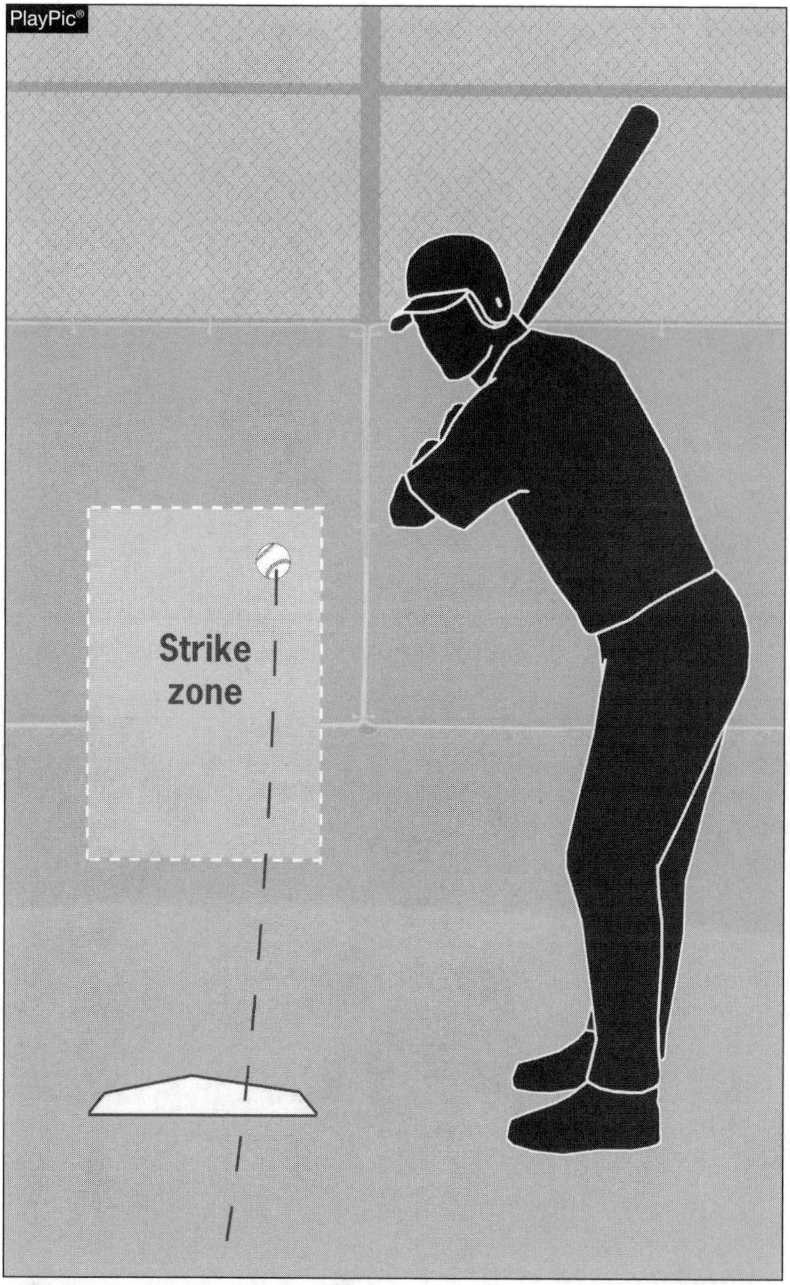

7-2-1a A strike is charged to the batter when a pitch enters any part of the strike zone in flight and is not struck at.

7-2-1b Even though the batter was hit by this pitch, he struck at the pitch and is charged with a strike.

7-2-1c A foul ball is charged as a strike to the batter when he has less than two strikes.

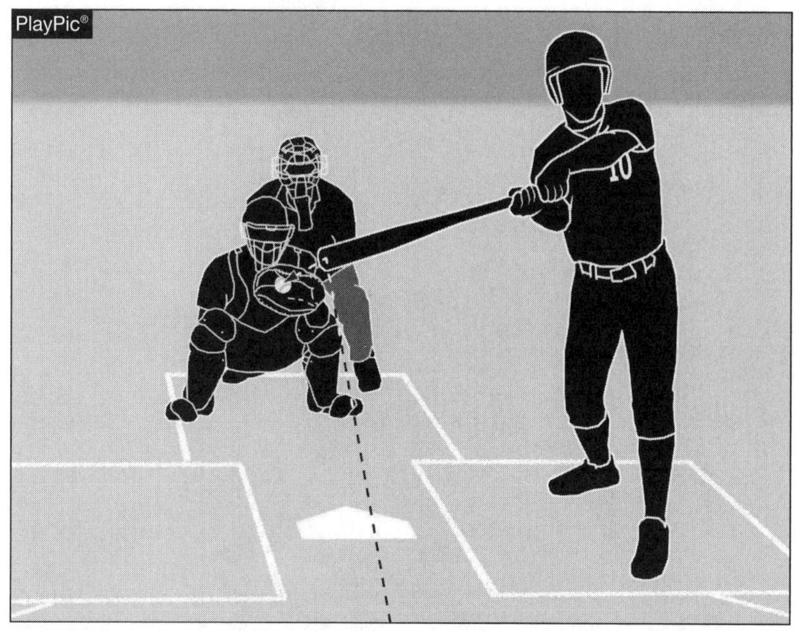

7-2-1d A foul tip is treated the same as a swinging strike (even on third strike).

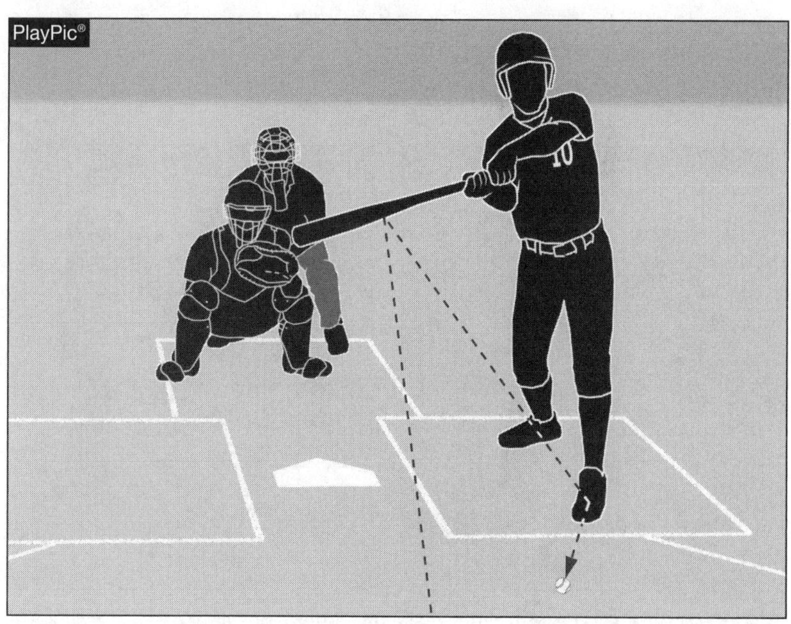

7-2-1f The ball is ruled foul and a strike is charged to the batter when a batted ball contacts the batter in the batter's box.

7-3-1 The batter must keep at least one foot in the batter's box while receiving his signs from the third base coach.

7-3-1 Exception A The batter may leave the batter's box after he swings at a pitch and misses.

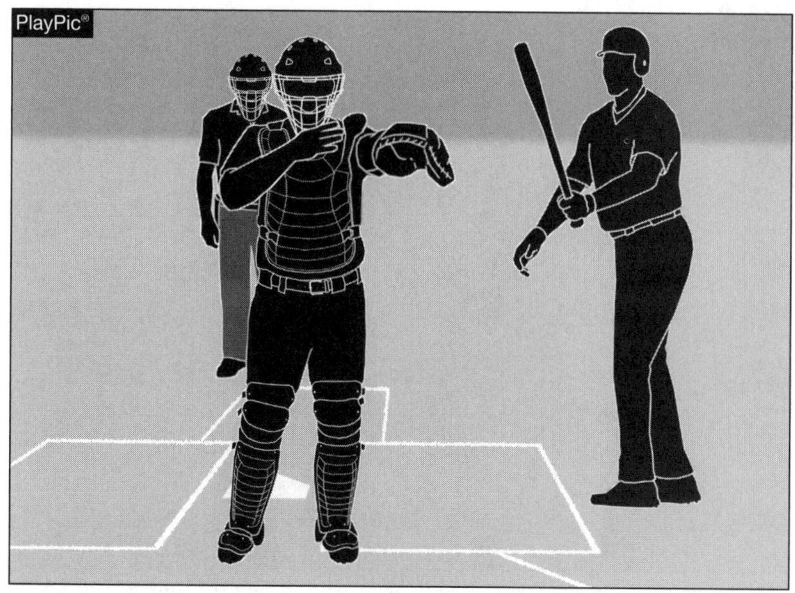

7-3-1 Exception G The batter may leave the batter's box when the catcher leaves the catcher's box to adjust his equipment or give defensive signals.

7-3-2 Both batters have illegally hit the ball. In PlayPic 1, the batter's front foot is entirely outside the box when he makes contact with the ball. In PlayPic 2, the batter's back foot is touching the plate. A batter may not touch the plate when he makes contact with the ball, even if part of his foot is in the batter's box.

7-3-3 A batter shall not disconcert the pitcher by stepping from the box on one side of the plate to the box on the other side while the pitcher is in position ready to pitch.

7-3-4 If the batter permits a pitch to touch him, the ball is dead, the batter remains at bat and the pitch is ruled a ball or strike. If the pitch is ball four, the batter walks (PlayPic 1). If the pitch is strike three, the batter is out (PlayPic 2).

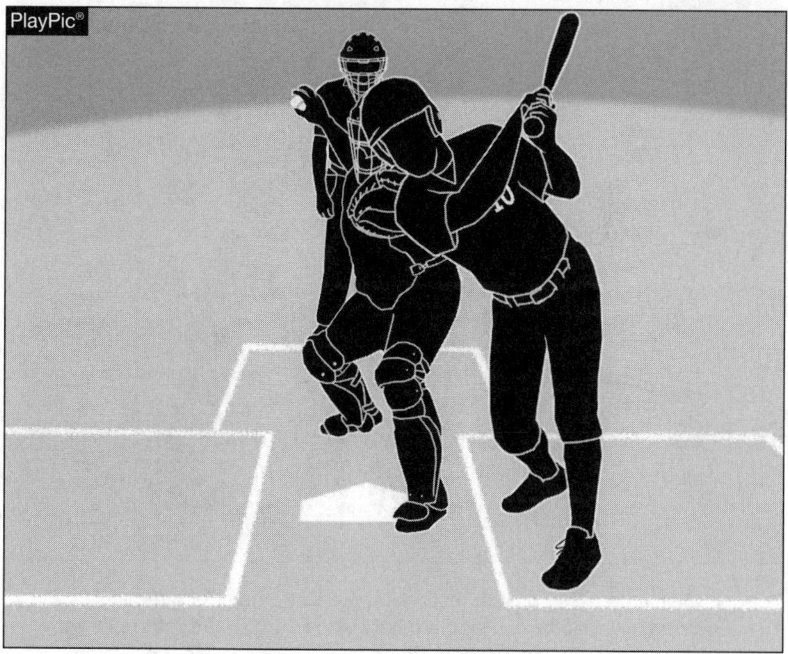

7-3-5 The batter has committed interference by leaning over the plate on his follow-through and impeding the catcher's ability to throw.

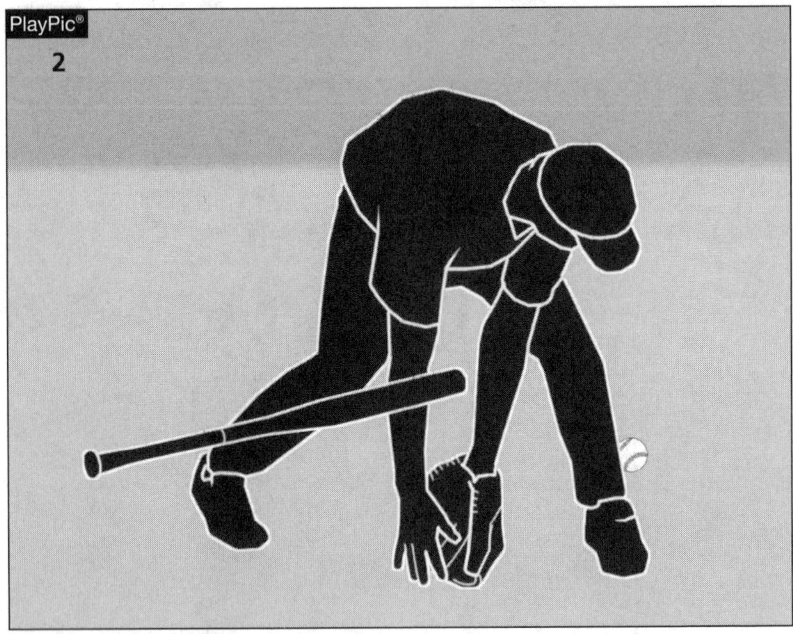

7-3-6 If the bat breaks and is hit by the ball or hits a runner or a fielder (PlayPic 1), no interference shall be called. If a whole bat is thrown and interferes with a defensive player attempting a play (PlayPic 2), interference has occurred and shall be called.

7-4-1a A batter is out when the batter enters the batter's box with an illegal bat (see 1-3-5) or is properly discovered having used an illegal bat. This batter is declared out for attempting to use a bat that has a -4 weight/length ratio. The head coach faces penalties when his player uses an illegal bat. See Rule 4-1-3b.

7-4-1b With a runner on first and less than two outs, the batter is out when a third strike is not caught. If there are two outs or if no runner occupies first base, the batter is not out unless the third strike is caught. He is entitled to try to reach first base before being tagged or thrown out.

7-4-1d A batter is out when a foul ball (other than a foul tip not a third strike) is caught by a fielder or such catch is prevented by a spectator reaching into the playing area (8-3-3e Exception).

7-4-1e A batter is out when an attempt to bunt on third strike is a foul.

7-4-1f When a coach/player interferes with the third baseman, who is attempting to field a foul fly ball, the batter is out and the ball is dead.

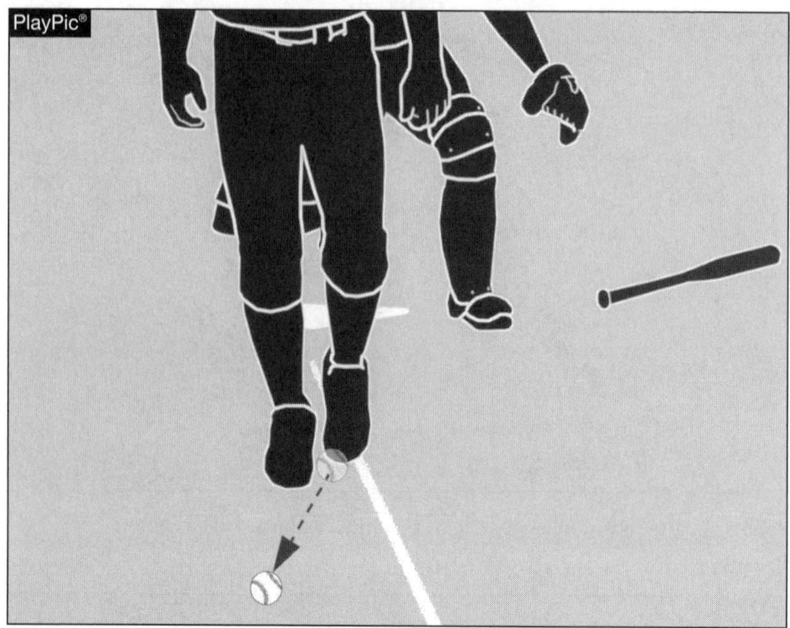

7-4-1i A batter is out when he intentionally deflects a foul ball which has a chance of becoming fair.

Part 3
Rule 8

Baserunning

A batter becomes a runner when his time at the plate has been completed. Once that happens, he is no longer covered by the previous rules involving a batter, but instead this rule, which governs the actions of a runner.

This rule covers a runner's advance around the bases, including the legal touching and occupation of bases and what steps the defense must take to appeal a runner missing a base or leaving a base on a caught fly ball before the ball was first touched.

There are a number of circumstances which cause a runner to be awarded bases, from one base for a balk to four bases for a ball going out of play over the fence in fair territory. Not only does this rule spell out all of the awards, but it designates the spot from which the award(s) will be made.

Lastly, this rule covers what causes the runner to be out — whether it is from the defense making a play to cause the out, or the runner doing something illegal such as making an illegal slide or causing interference.

8-1-1d A batter may not permit himself to be touched by a pitched ball. It is irrelevant whether the batter attempted to move out of the path of the pitch, but he is required by rule not to allow the ball to touch him.

8-1-1e The batter's swing is obstructed by the catcher. The batter shall be awarded first base unless the coach chooses to take the result of the play. Obstruction is ignored if the batter and all other runners advance one base on the play.

8-1-1e The catcher may not obstruct or impede the batter. The batter is awarded first base, and any runner attempting to advance (i.e. steal or squeeze) shall be awarded the base he is attempting.

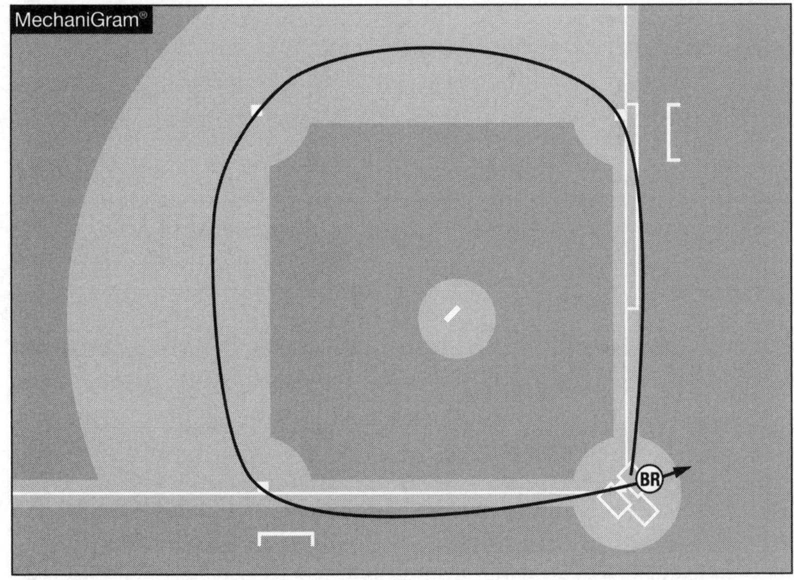

8-2-1 An advancing runner shall touch first, second, third and then the plate in order, including awarded bases.

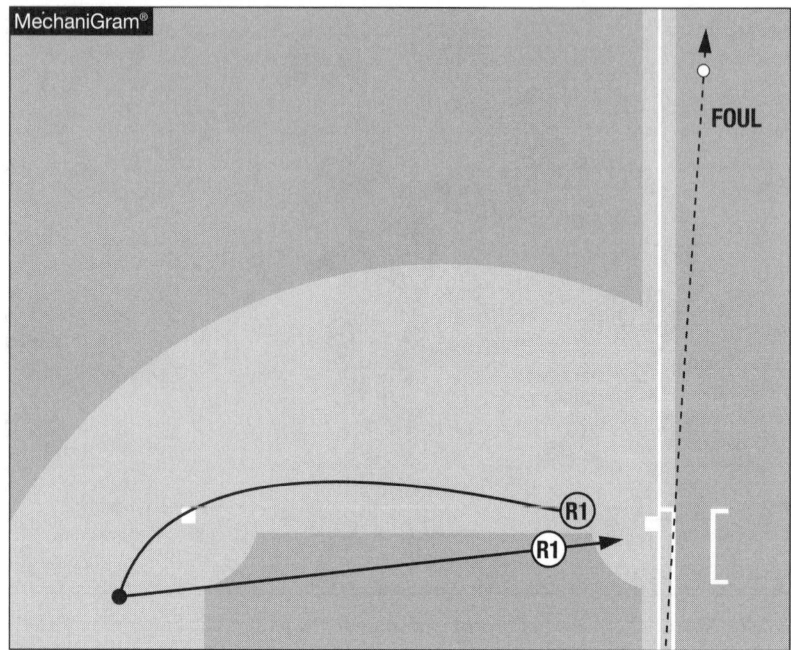

8-2-2 When returning to his base after an uncaught foul, it is not necessary for a returning runner to retouch intervening bases. The umpire will not make the ball live until the runner returns to the appropriate base.

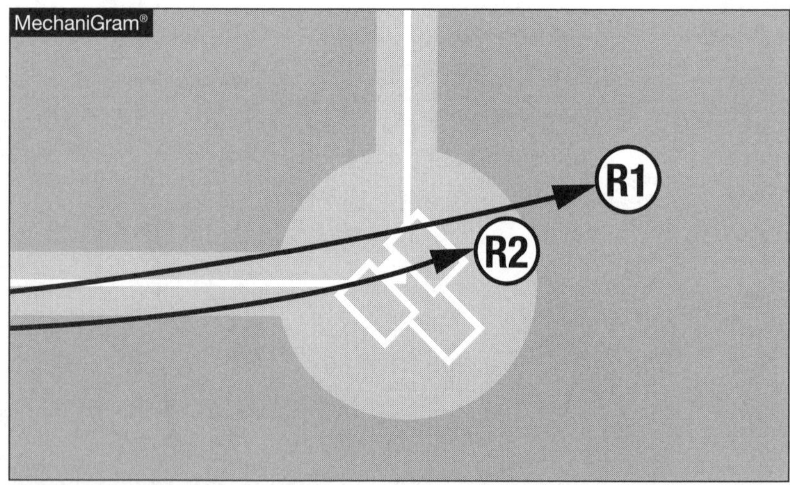

8-2-3 R1 advances past, but does not touch, the plate. R2 then scores by touching the plate. At that point, R1 may not legally return to touch the plate and shall be called out after a proper appeal.

8-2-4 Before advancing on a batted ball that is legally caught, the runner must touch his base after the ball has touched a fielder. If the runner fails to do so, he may be called out on proper appeal.

8-2-5 Once a runner misses any base (including the plate) or leaves a base too early, he must return to touch the base immediately. If the ball becomes dead and the runner is on or beyond a succeeding base, he cannot return to the missed base and, therefore, is subject to being declared out upon proper appeal.

8-2-6b An appeal may be made during a live ball by any fielder in possession of the ball by touching the base in question or by tagging the runner who committed the violation, if the runner is still on the field.

8-2-6c The fielder does not need the ball to make a dead-ball appeal.

8-2-6h If a runner leaves a base too soon on a caught fly ball and returns in an attempt to retag (PlayPic 1), this is a time play and not a force out. If the appeal is the third out, all runs scored by runners in advance of the appealed runner and scored ahead of the legal appeal would count (PlayPic 2).

8-2-6j If any situation arises which could lead to an appeal by the defense on the last play of the game, the appeal must be made while an umpire is still on the field of play.

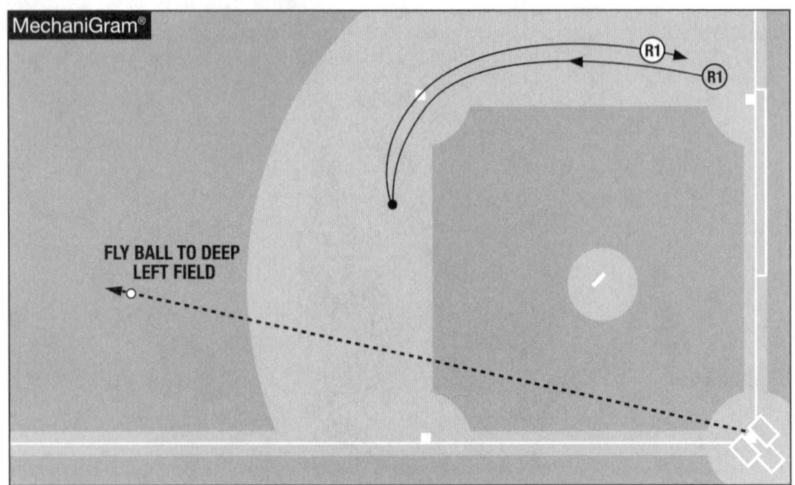

8-2-6l A player who touches a base on the last time by cannot be called out on appeal. In the above MechaniGram, R1 misses second while advancing, but touches it while returning once the fly ball is caught. R1 is not subject to being called out by appeal.

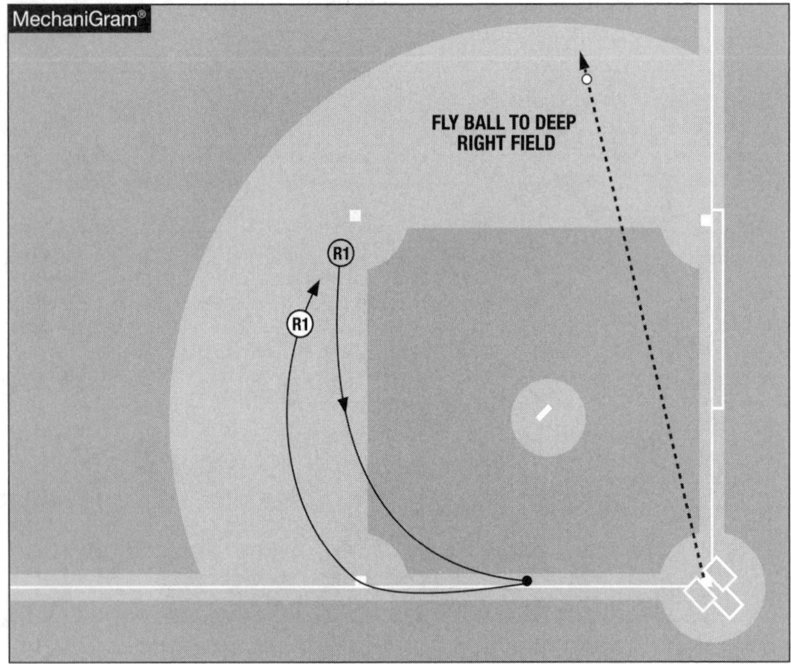

8-2-6l R1 intentionally tries to circumvent the "last time by" rule by cutting off a large margin around third base. Even though he touched it on his "last time by," he is subject to being called out on appeal for his intentional unsporting act.

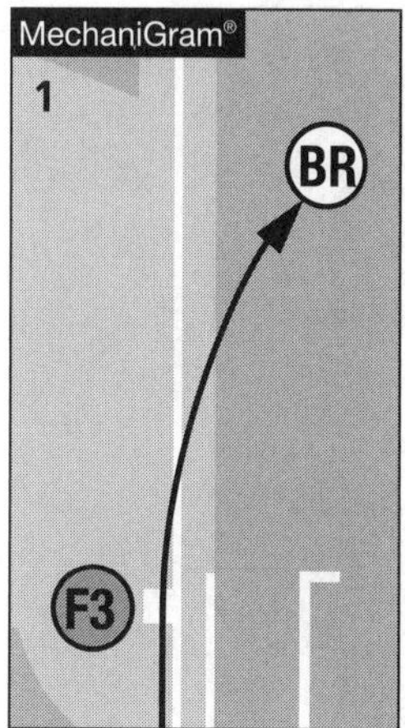

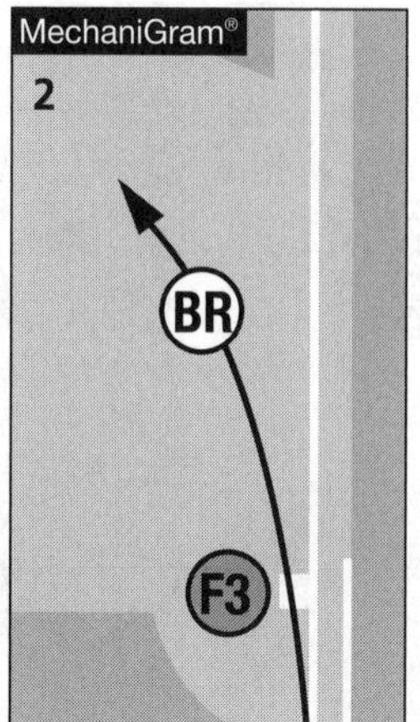

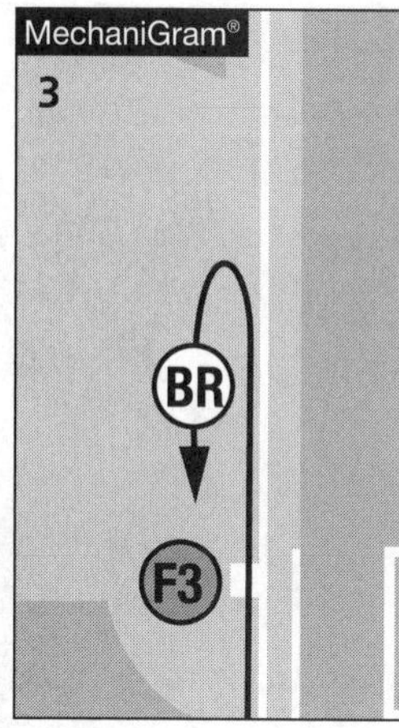

8-2-7 A batter-runner who reaches first base safely and then overruns or overslides may immediately return without liability of being put out provided he does not attempt or feint an advance to second. The runner in MechaniGram 1 is not liable to be put out, while the runner in MechaniGram 2 would be in jeopardy. Turning around while in fair territory (MechaniGram 3) is not an attempt or feint.

8-2-8 A runner does not have to vacate his base to permit a fielder to catch a fly ball in the infield, but he may not interfere (PlayPic 1). By being off the bag, the runner in PlayPic 2 has definitely interfered with the fielder.

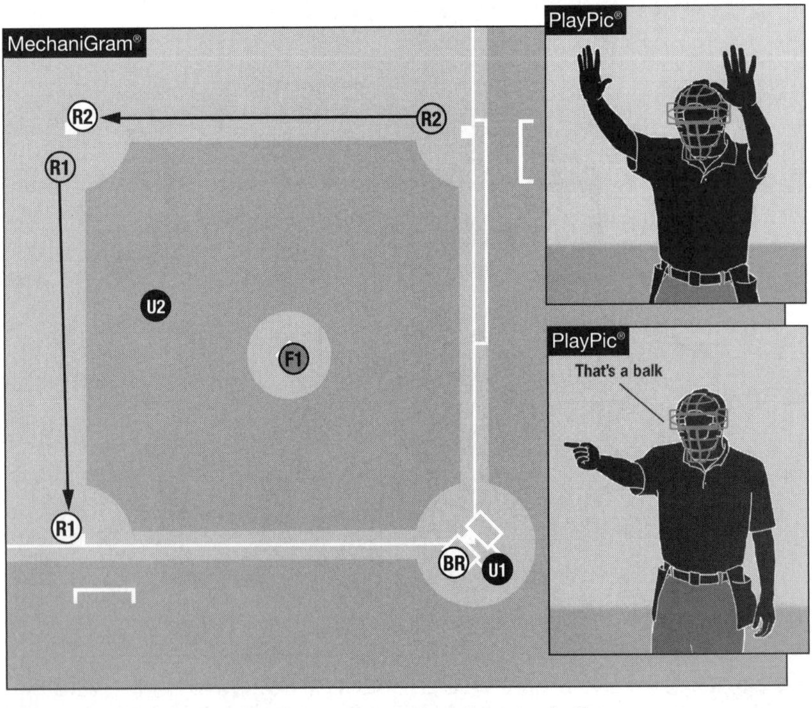

8-3-1a Each runner is awarded one base when there is a balk.

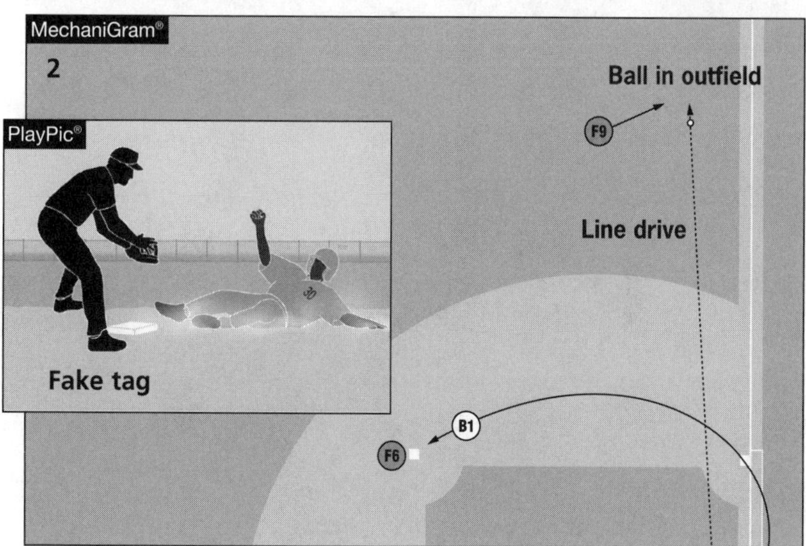

8-3-2 When a runner is obstructed by a fielder without the ball (PlayPic 1) or by a fielder without the ball faking a tag (MechaniGram 2), the umpire shall call obstruction (PlayPic 3) which is a delayed-dead ball (PlayPic 4). An obstructed runner and all other runners affected are awarded the bases they would have reached, in the umpire's opinion, had there been no obstruction. If the runner achieves the base he was attempting to acquire, then the obstruction is ignored. The obstructed runner is awarded a minimum of one base beyond his position on base when the obstruction occurred.

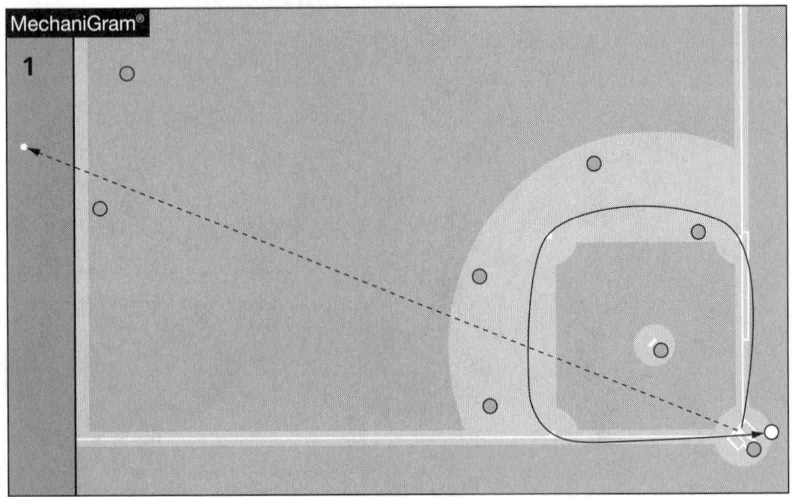

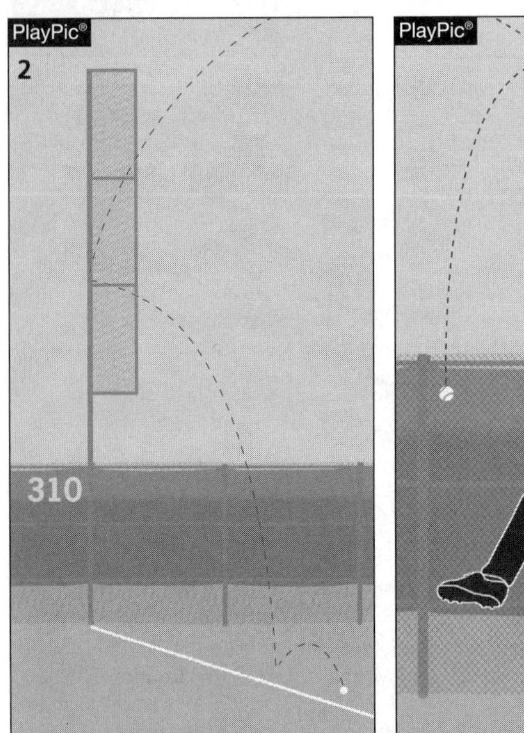

8-3-3a The batter's fair batted ball goes out of the park in flight (MechaniGram 1), hits a foul pole above the fence (PlayPic 2), or is prevented from going over by being touched by detached player equipment which is thrown, tossed, kicked or held by a fielder (PlayPic 3). In each case, the batter and all runners are awarded four bases.

8-3-3b When a fielder throws his glove at and hits a fair batted ball or a batted ball that has a chance to become fair, each runner, including the batter-runner, is awarded three bases from the time of the infraction. That is a delayed dead-ball situation and the batter-runner is liable to be put out if he attempts to score on the play.

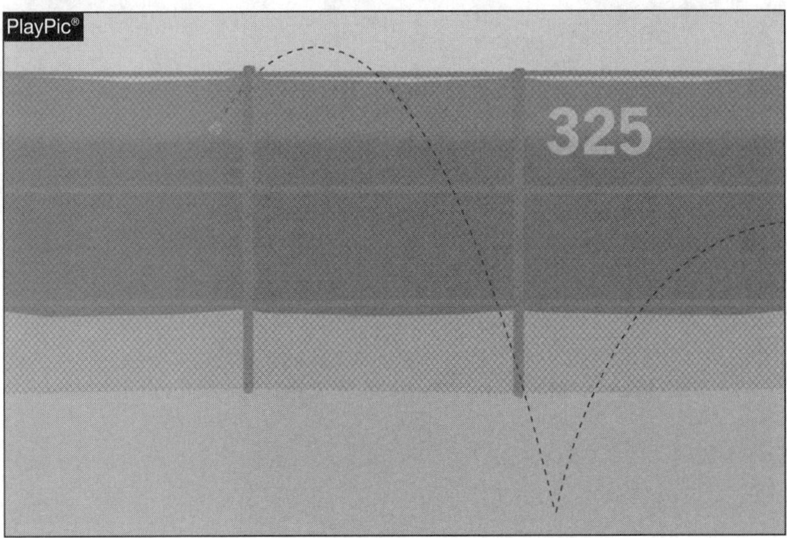

8-3-3c Each runner is awarded two bases if a fair batted ball bounces over or passes through a fence.

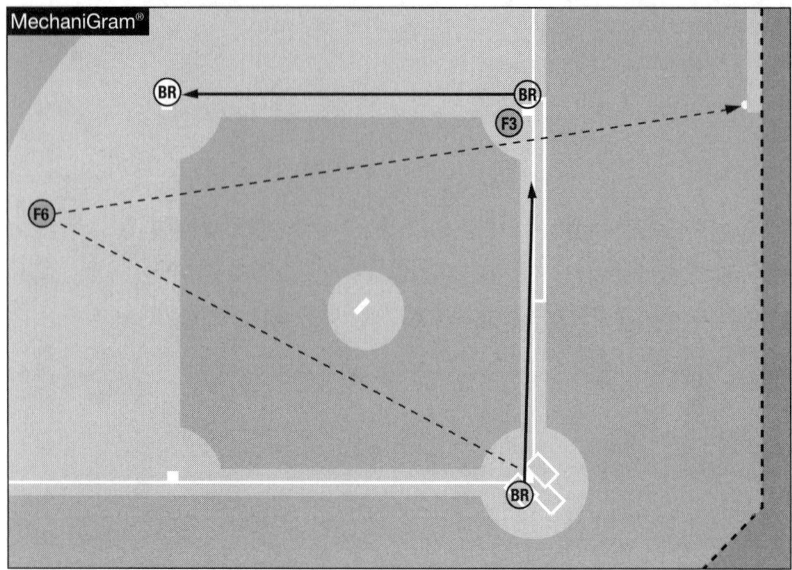

8-3-3c Each runner is awarded two bases if a live thrown ball goes into a stand for spectators, dugout or player's bench or over or through or lodges in a fence and it is not thrown by a pitcher from his plate. On this play, the batter-runner would be awarded second base.

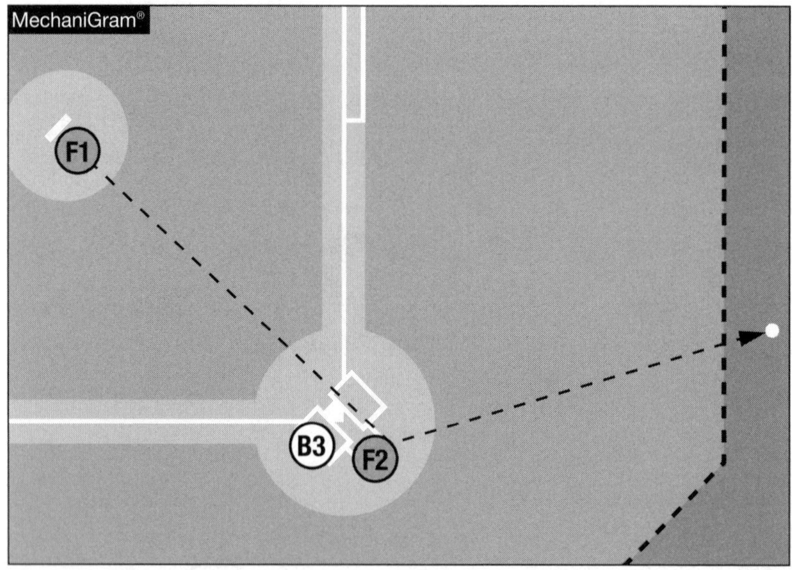

8-3-3d Each runner is awarded one base if a pitch or any throw by the pitcher from his pitching position on his plate goes into dead-ball territory.

8-3-3d When the ball lodges in a catcher's equipment, the ball is dead and each runner is awarded one base.

8-3-3d When a fielder with the ball leaves the field of play by stepping with both feet into dead-ball territory, each runner is awarded one base. If the fielder's catch is the third out, no award is made.

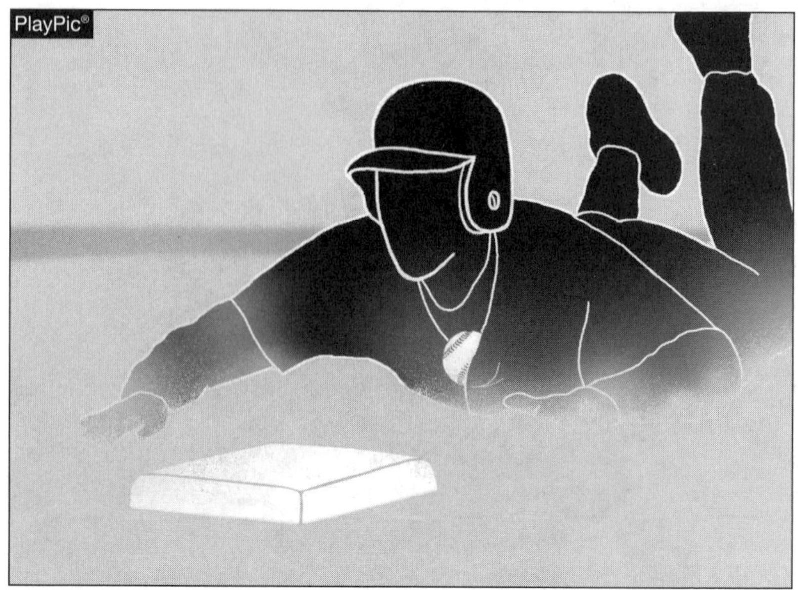

8-3-3f When the ball becomes lodged in an offensive player's uniform, each runner is awarded one base beyond his last legally acquired base, if in the umpire's judgment the runner was attempting to advance at the time.

8-3-6 When the plate umpire hinders, impedes or prevents a catcher's throw attempting to prevent a stolen base or to retire a runner on a pickoff play, if an out is not made at the end of the catcher's initial throw, the ball shall be dead and all runners shall return to the bases occupied at the time of the interference.

8-4-1a The batter-runner is out when he intentionally interferes with the catcher's attempt to field the ball after a third strike.

8-4-1b The batter-runner is out when his fair hit or foul is caught by a fielder.

8-4-1c The batter-runner is out when his fair fly is intentionally dropped by an infielder with at least first base occupied and before there are two outs. The ball is dead and the runner or runners shall return to their respective base(s).

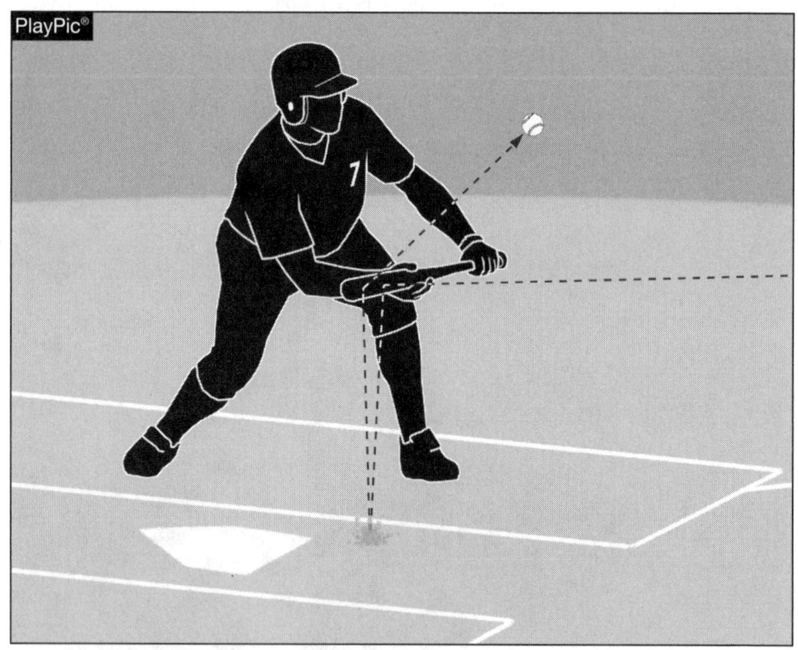

8-4-1d The batter-runner is out when he intentionally contacts the ball with the bat a second time in fair territory. The ball is dead and no runner(s) advance. Exception: If the bat and ball accidentally come in contact with each other a second time while the batter is holding the bat in the batter's box, it is a foul ball.

8-4-1e The batter is out if the third strike is not caught with first base occupied and less than two outs.

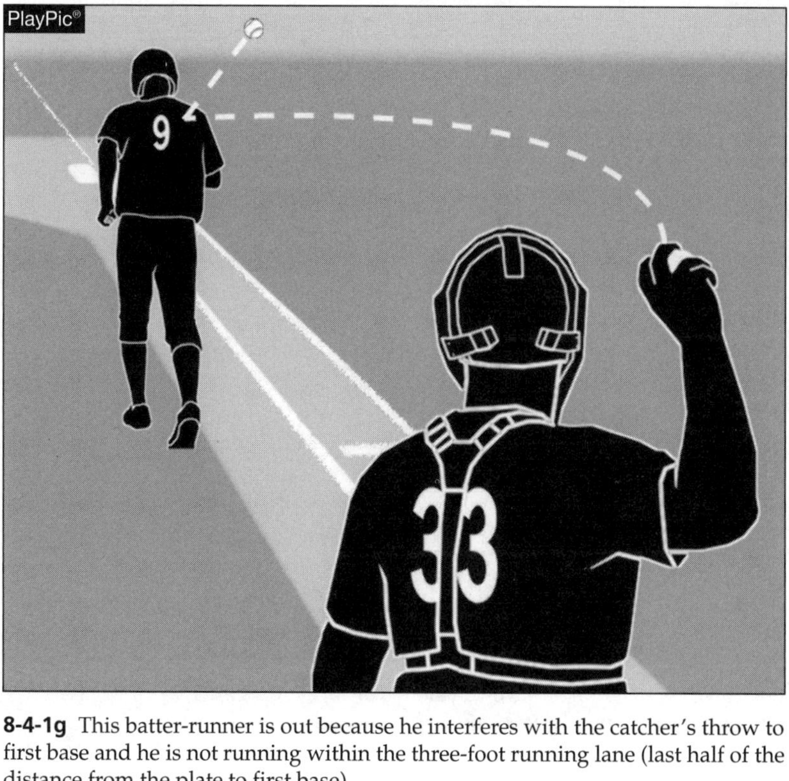

8-4-1g This batter-runner is out because he interferes with the catcher's throw to first base and he is not running within the three-foot running lane (last half of the distance from the plate to first base).

8-4-1i When the third strike on a batter is dropped, the batter is out when he gives up by entering the bench or dugout area.

8-4-2a The runner is out because he has run more than three feet away from a direct line between bases to avoid a tag.

8-4-2b Any runner is out when he does not legally slide and causes illegal contact and/or illegally alters the actions of a fielder in the immediate act of making a play. This slide is illegal because the runner's leg is higher than the fielder's knee.

8-4-2b Exception A runner may slide in a direction away from the fielder to avoid making contact or altering the play of the fielder.

8-4-2c This runner is out (for interference) because he did not avoid the fielder who is in the immediate act of making a play.

8-4-2d Any runner is out when he dives over a fielder.

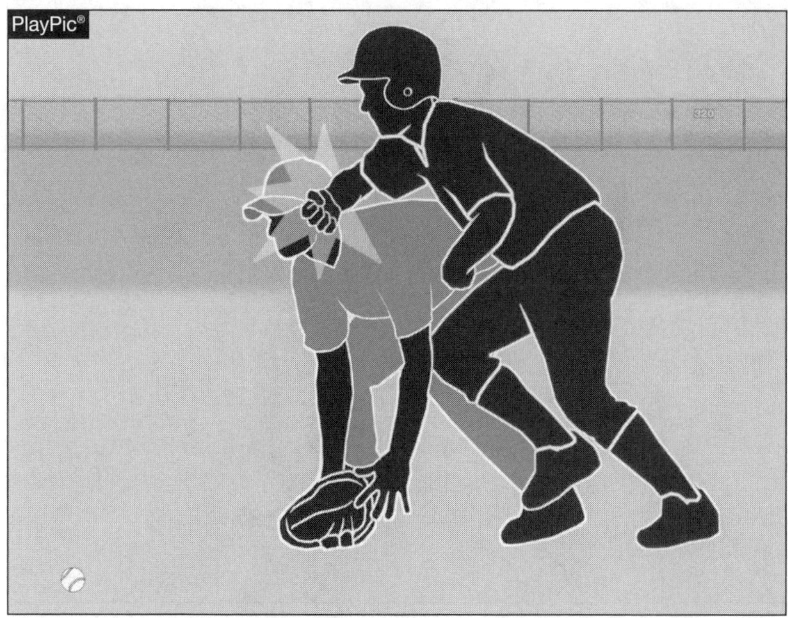

8-4-2e Any runner is out when he initiates malicious contact. When malicious contact by the offense occurs, the runner is out (unless he has already scored), the runner is ejected and all other runners return to the last base touched at the time of the malicious contact.

8-4-2f This runner is out because he failed to execute a legal slide. This slide is illegal because he slid past the bag and made contact with the fielder.

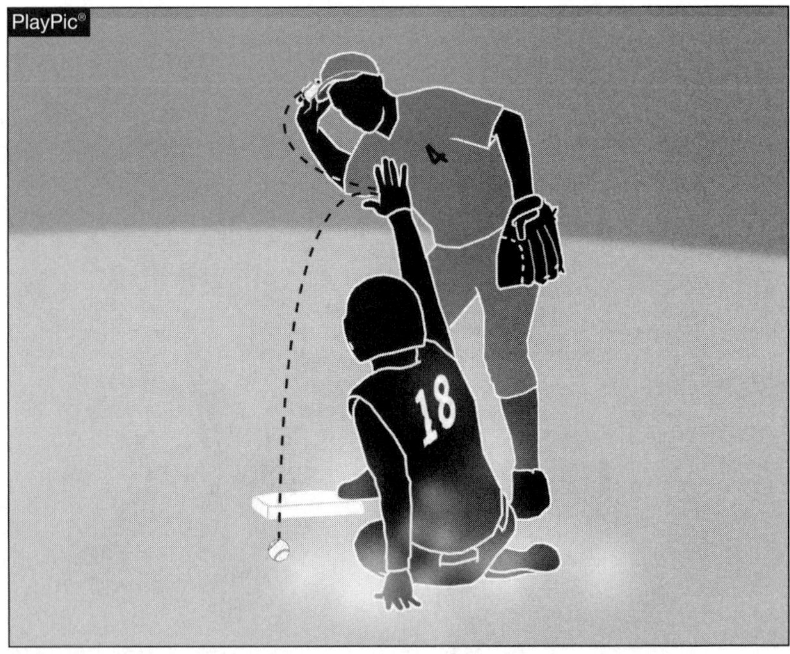

8-4-2g Any runner is out when he intentionally interferes with a throw. If, in the judgment of the umpire, the runner's actions prevents a double play, two outs shall be called (the runner who interfered and the other runner involved).

8-4-2j When a fielder has caught the ball while touching the base before a runner has arrived, the runner is out if his advance was forced because the batter became a runner. In this case, the batter-runner is out because the fielder with the ball touched first base before the runner.

8-4-2k This runner is out because he was hit by a fair batted ball before it touched or passed the infielder.

8-4-2l With less than two outs, the runner is out when he attempts to advance to home when the batter interferes with the catcher. With two outs, the batter is out and the runner cannot score.

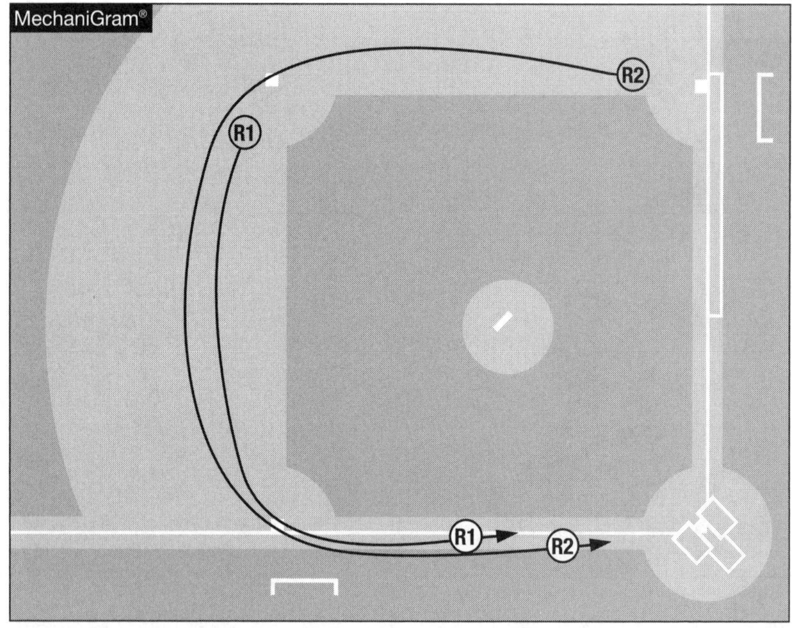

8-4-2m As long as R1 was not obstructed, R2 is out for passing R1.

8-4-2o Any runner is out when he positions himself behind a base to get a running start.

8-4-2r Any runner is out when he deliberately knocks the ball from a fielder's hand.

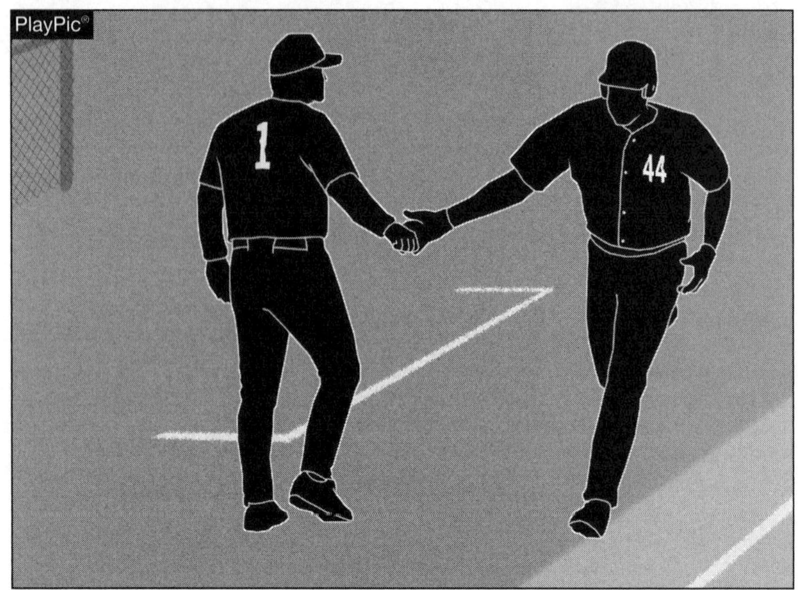

8-4-2s A coach congratulating a runner is not physically assisting a runner. There is no violation.

Part 3

Rule 9 & 10

Scoring – Record Keeping and Umpiring

Most of Rule 9 deals with the procedures and rules for maintaining the scorebook and statistical record from a game or season. However, the first part of the rule is one of the most essential in the game — how and when a run scores. It also explains that even though a runner crosses the plate, a run does not score when the third out occurs in any of five different ways.

The final rule in the book deals with the umpires, and the duties and responsibilities they have in enforcing the game's other rules. This rule lists the responsibilities that belong to any of the officials in the game, and then specifically those that belong to the umpire-in-chief and those that are reserved for the field umpire(s).

Finally, after Rule 10, there is a section of "Suggested Speed-Up Rules." These are rules that can be used if the state association adopts them, either in part or in total. Their purpose is to help maintain the pace of the game by eliminating or reducing delays that can occur.

9-1-1 A runner scores one run each time he legally advances to and touches first, second, third and then the plate before there are three outs to end the inning.

A run is not scored if the runner advances to the plate during action in which the third out is made:

a. by the batter-runner before he touches first base.

b. by another runner being forced out.

c. by a preceding runner who is declared out upon appeal.

d. during a play in which an umpire observed a baserunning infraction resulting in a force-out.

e. when there is more than one out declared by the umpire which terminates the half inning, the defensive team may select the out which is to its advantage.

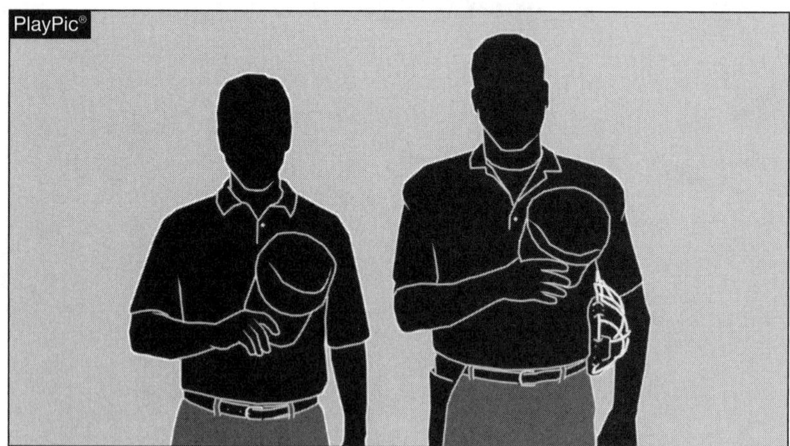

10-1-1 Game officials include the umpire-in-chief and one, two, three or more field umpires. Whenever possible, at least two umpires are recommended.

10-1-2 Umpire jurisdiction begins upon the umpires arriving within confines of the field and ends when the umpires leave the playing field at the conclusion of the game.

10-1-2 The game officials retain clerical authority over the contest through the completion of any reports, including those imposing disqualification, that are responsive to actions occurring while the umpires had jurisdiction.

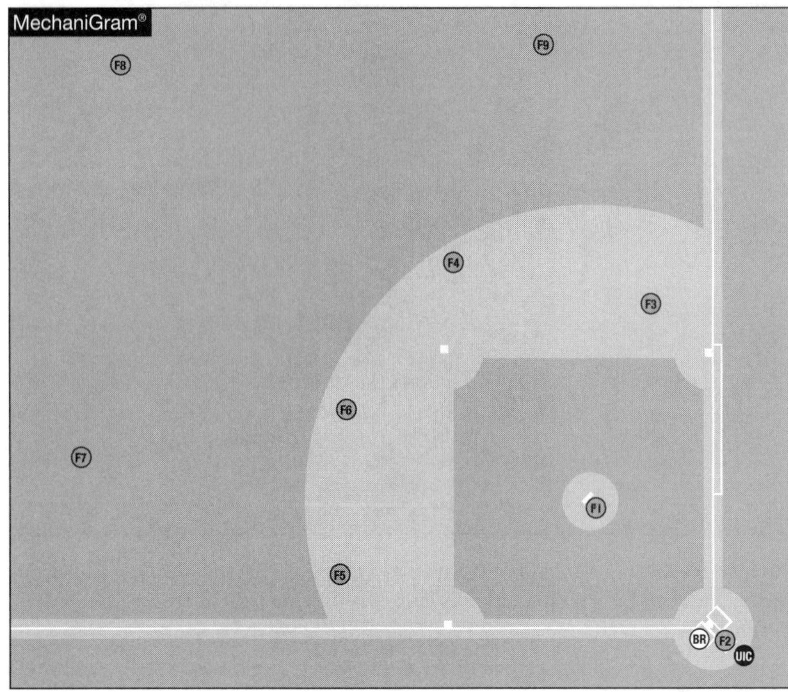

10-1-3 If there is only one umpire, he has complete jurisdiction in administering the rules and he may take any position he desires, preferably behind the catcher.

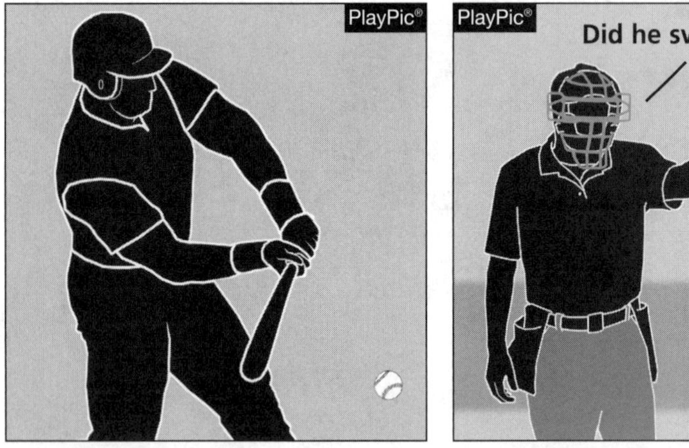

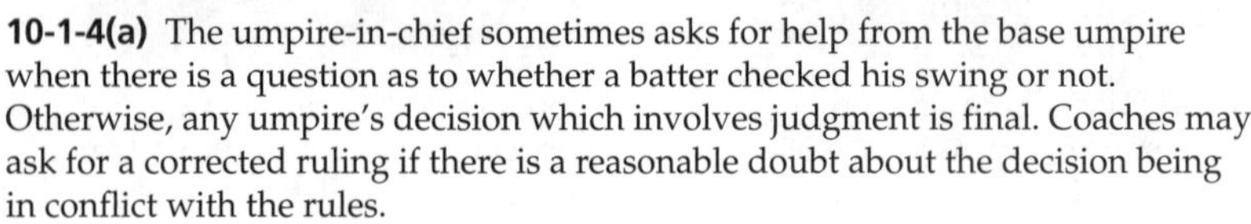
10-1-4(a) The umpire-in-chief sometimes asks for help from the base umpire when there is a question as to whether a batter checked his swing or not. Otherwise, any umpire's decision which involves judgment is final. Coaches may ask for a corrected ruling if there is a reasonable doubt about the decision being in conflict with the rules.

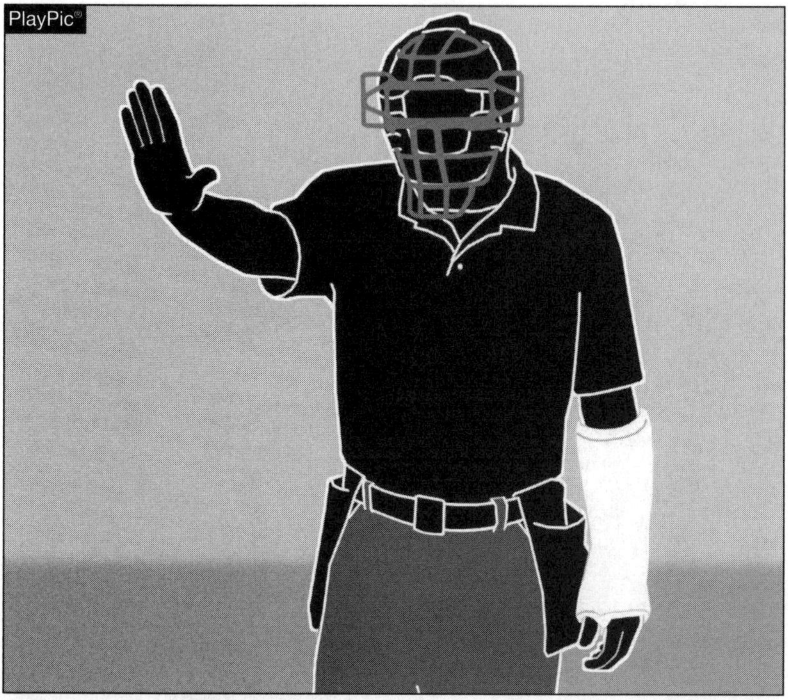

PlayPic®

10-1-7 Casts, splints and braces may be worn, if padded. Umpires may wear prostheses and use mobility devices.

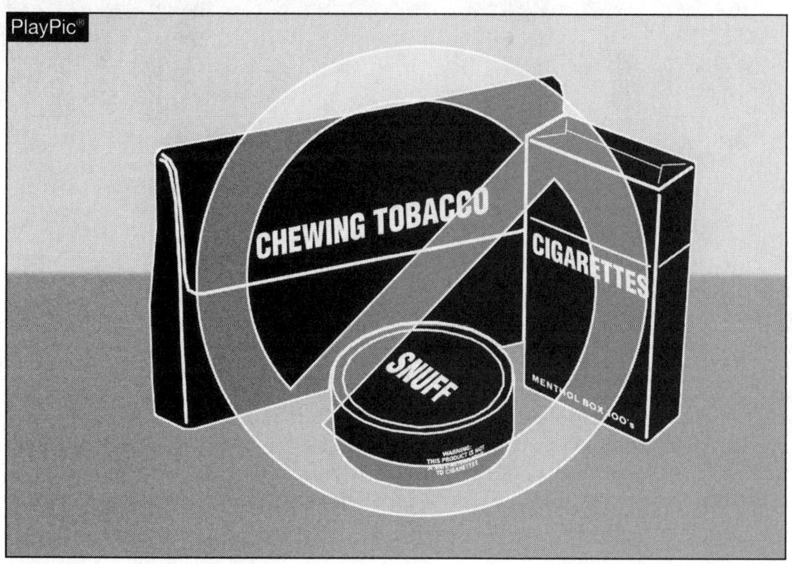

10-1-8 Umpires shall not use tobacco or tobacco-like products on or in the vicinity of the playing field.

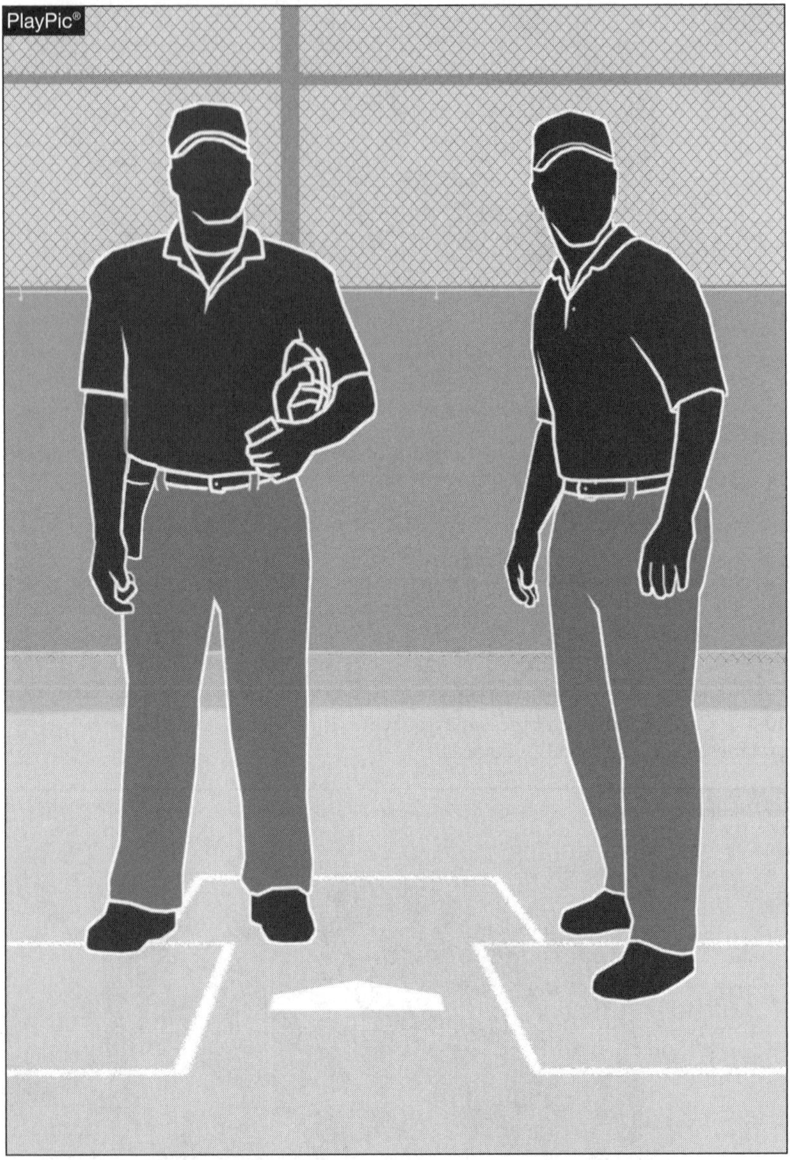

10-1-9 The uniform for umpires is a navy blue shirt and gray slacks. Umpires are no longer required to wear heather gray slacks. By state association adoption, umpires may wear other color shirts, as long as all umpires are wearing the same color. Umpires must still strive to look professional and not wear uniforms that are dirty, faded, wrinkled or torn.

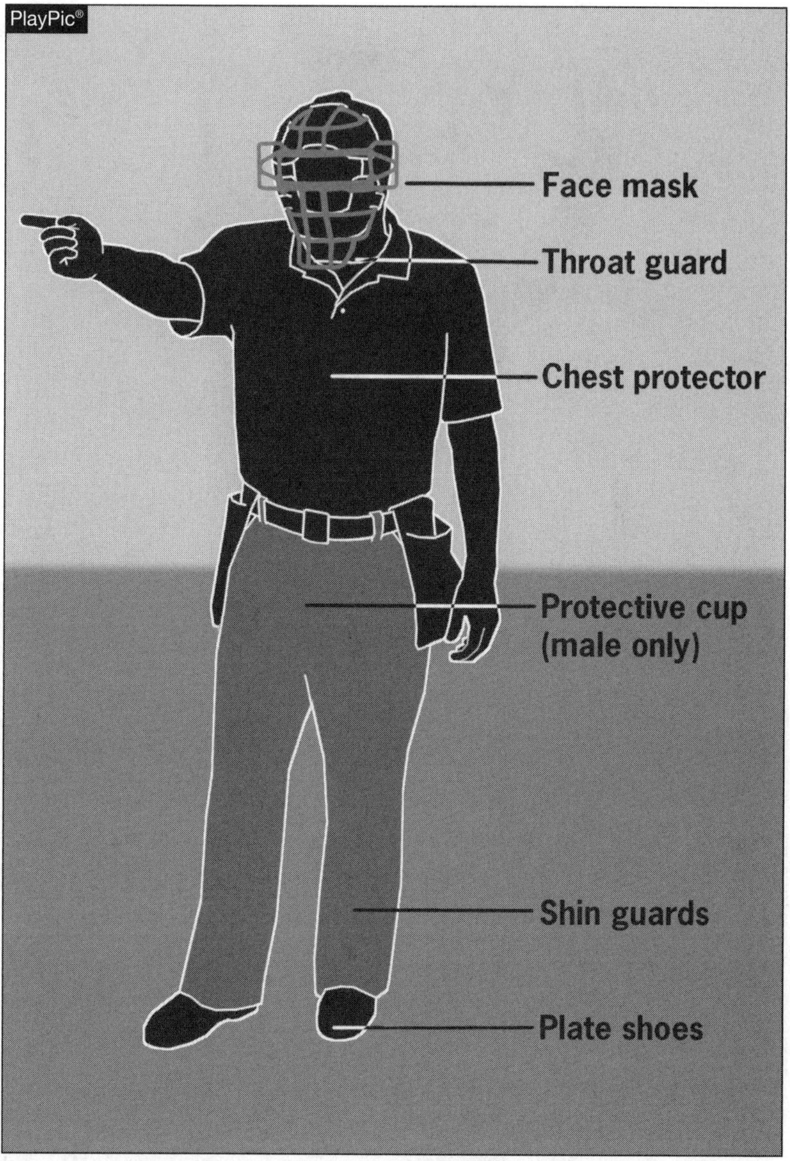

10-2-1 The plate umpire shall wear the following required equipment for his protection. The throat guard does not have to be a separate dangling piece, but may be attached to the mask, as shown here.

PlayPic®

10-2-2 The umpire-in-chief has sole authority to forfeit a game and has jurisdiction over any rules matters not assigned to the field umpire.

10-2-3c If it becomes necessary, the umpire-in chief's duties include ejecting or restricting a coach or player.

10-2-3j The umpire-in chief must keep a written record of defensive and offensive team charged conferences for each team. He shall also record all substitutes, courtesy runner participation, and team warnings.

10-2-3j Umpires will issue a written warning to coaches for any minor offense.

10-2-3n Umpires have the responsibility of ordering the lights turned on whenever they believe darkness could make further play hazardous. Whenever possible, lights should be turned on at the beginning of an inning.

Suggested Speed-up Rules
(By State Adoption)

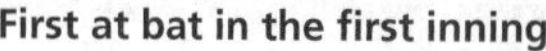
First at bat in the first inning

Second at bat in the first inning

Optional Speed-Up Rules: Courtesy Runner No. 44 is the courtesy runner for the catcher, No. 2. If his team bats around in an inning, No. 2 has not been substituted for and may bat when it is his turn.

First at bat in the first inning

Second at bat in the first inning

Optional Speed-Up Rules: Courtesy Runner If the offense bats around and No. 2 reaches base a second time in the inning, he may run for himself and is not required to be replaced by a courtesy runner.

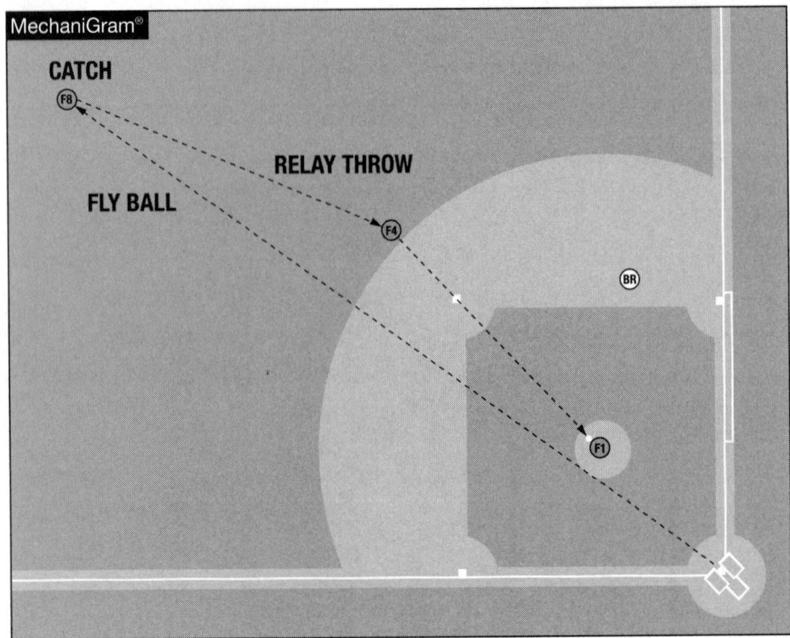

AFTER PUTOUTS After a putout in the outfield and with no runners on base, the ball shall be thrown to a cutoff man and, if desired, to one additional infielder before being returned to the pitcher for delivery to the next batter.

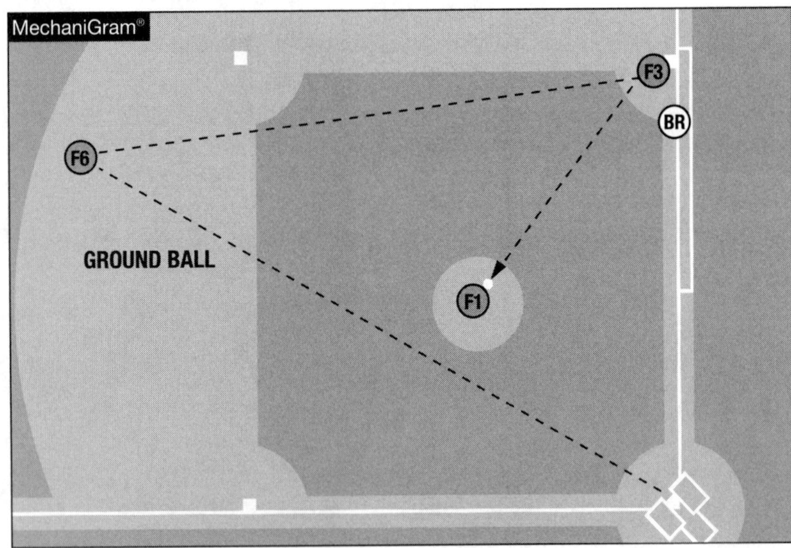

AFTER PUTOUTS After a putout in the infield and with no runners on base, the ball shall be returned directly to the pitcher.

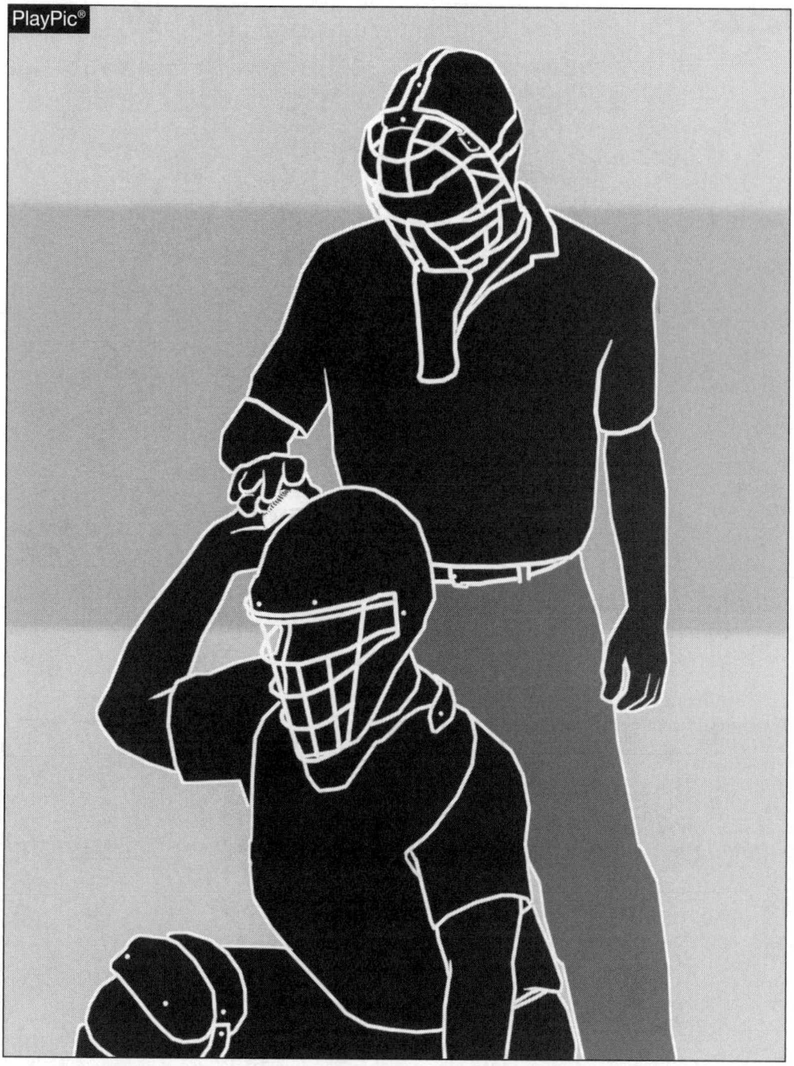

PlayPic®

AFTER PUTOUTS Following the final out in any inning, the ball shall be given to the nearest umpire. The plate umpire shall then give the ball to the catcher. The base umpire shall place the ball on the pitcher's plate.

SUGGESTED DOUBLE FIRST BASE RULES With a double first base, the runner is required to use the colored base while the fielder uses the white portion.

SUGGESTED DOUBLE FIRST BASE RULES On a dropped third strike that rolls into foul territory, the fielder is permitted to use the colored base to record the out, while the runner is permitted to use the white base.

Signal Chart

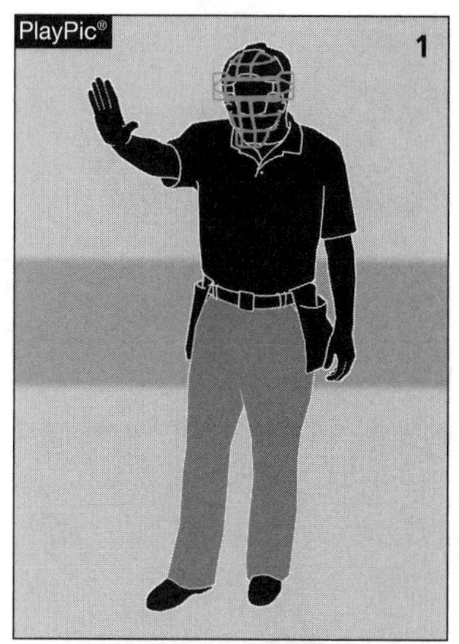

Do Not Pitch; Ball Is Dead

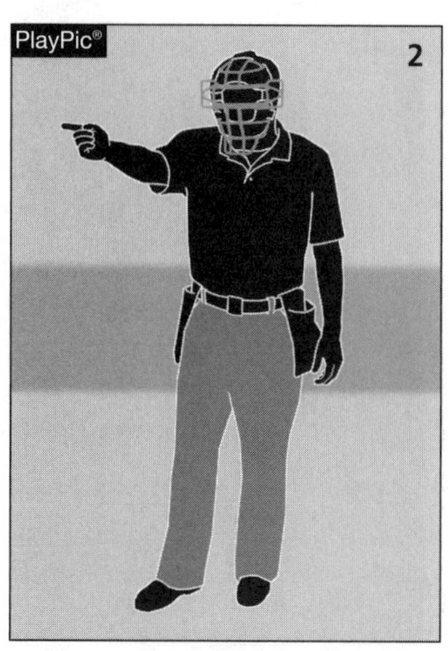

Play

Strike

Foul Tip

Infield Fly

Foul Ball, Time Out Or Dead Ball

Fair Ball

Out

Safe

Count

Time play

Double Tag Rotation

NFHS PUBLICATIONS

Prices effective April 1, 2017 — March 31, 2018

RULES PUBLICATIONS

Baseball Rules Book.....$10.00
Baseball Case Book.....$10.00
Baseball Umpires Manual (2017 & 2018).....$10.00
Baseball Simplified & Illustrated Rules.....$10.00
Baseball Rules by Topic.....$10.00
Basketball Rules Book.....$10.00
Basketball Case Book.....$10.00
Basketball Simplified & Illustrated Rules.....$10.00
Basketball Officials Manual (2017-19).....$10.00
Basketball Handbook (2016-18).....$10.00
Basketball Rules by Topic.....$10.00
Field Hockey Rules Book.....$10.00
Football Rules Book.....$10.00
Football Case Book.....$10.00
Football Simplified & Illustrated Rules.....$10.00
Football Handbook (2017 & 2018).....$10.00
Football Game Officials Manual (2016 & 2017).....$10.00
Football Rules by Topic.....$10.00
Girls Gymnastics Rules Book & Manual (2016-18).....$10.00
Ice Hockey Rules Book.....$10.00
Boys Lacrosse Rules Book.....$10.00
Girls Lacrosse Rules Book.....$10.00
Soccer Rules Book.....$10.00
Softball Rules Book.....$10.00
Softball Case Book.....$10.00
Softball Umpires Manual (2018 & 2019).....$10.00
Softball Simplified & Illustrated Rules.....$10.00
Softball Rules by Topic.....$10.00
Spirit Rules Book.....$10.00
Swimming & Diving Rules Book.....$10.00
Track & Field Rules Book.....$10.00
Track & Field Case Book.....$10.00
Track & Field Manual (2017 & 2018).....$10.00
Volleyball Rules Book.....$10.00
Volleyball Case Book & Manual.....$10.00
Water Polo Rules Book.....$10.00
Wrestling Rules Book.....$10.00
Wrestling Case Book & Manual.....$10.00

MISCELLANEOUS ITEMS

NFHS Statisticians' Manual.....$8.00
Scorebooks: Baseball-Softball, Basketball, Swimming & Diving, Cross Country, Soccer, Track & Field, Gymnastics, Volleyball, Wrestling and Field Hockey.....$12.00
Diving Scoresheets (pad of 100).....$8.00
Volleyball Team Rosters & Lineup Sheets (pads of 100).....$8.00
Libero Tracking Sheet (pads of 50).....$8.00
Baseball/Softball Lineup Sheets – 3-Part NCR (sets/100).....$10.00
Wrestling Tournament Match Cards (sets/100).....$10.00
Competitors Numbers (Track and Gymnastics – Waterproof, nontearable, black numbers and six colors of backgrounds numbers are 1-1000 sold in sets of 100.....$15.00/set

MISCELLANEOUS SPORTS ITEMS

Court and Field Diagram Guide.....$25.00
NFHS Handbook (2016-17).....$12.00
Let's Make It Official.....$5.00
Sportsmanship. It's Up to You. Toolkit.....$19.95
High School Activities – A Community Investment in America.....$39.95

ORDERING

Individuals ordering NFHS publications and other products and materials are requested to order online at **www.nfhs.com**.

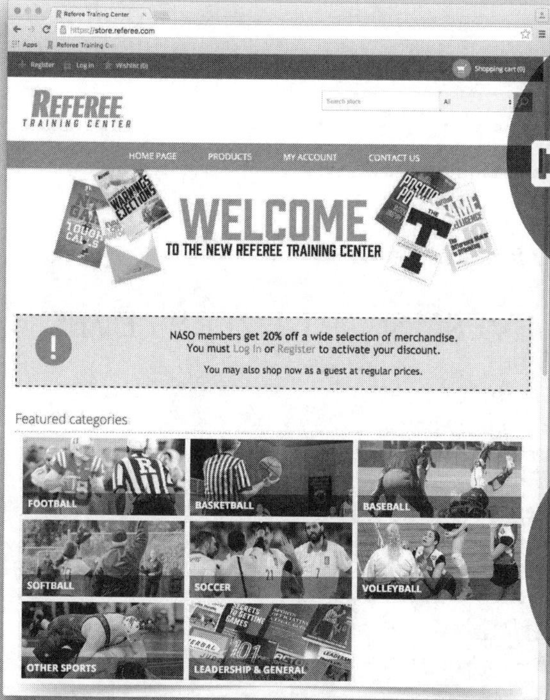